THE WORD BECAME FRESH

HOW TO PREACH FROM OLD TESTAMENT NARRATIVE TEXTS

Dale Ralph Davis

MENTOR

There is no more gifted expositor of the Old Testament in our day than Ralph Davis. His book not only brings scholarly research to bear on the subject, but also reflects his many years of preaching week after week through the OT. What a gift to the church to have such a fine book.

Dr Richard L. Pratt, Jr.
Adjunct Professor of Old Testament, Reformed Theological Seminary
President, Third Millennium Ministries

Scripture quotations marked RSV are taken from the *Revised Standard Version* of the Bible, copyright 1952 [2nd edition, 1971] by the Division of Christian Education of the National Council of the Churches of Christ in the United States of America. Used by permission. All rights reserved.

Scripture quotations marked ESV are from *The Holy Bible, English Standard Version*, copyright © 2001 by Crossway Bibles, a division of Good News Publishers. Used by permission. All rights reserved.

Scripture quotations marked NIV are taken from *the Holy Bible, New International Version*. NIV. Copyright©1973, 1978, 1984 by International Bible Society. Used by permission of Zondervan. All rights reserved.

© Dale Ralph Davis

ISBN 978-1-84550-192-1

10 9 8 7 6 5 4 3 2 1

Published in 2006
Reprinted 2007
by
Christian Focus Publications Ltd.,
Geanies House, Fearn, Tain,
Ross-shire, IV20 1TW, Scotland
www.christianfocus.com

Cover design by Danie Van Straaten
Printed and bound by Creative Print and Design, Wales

CONTENTS

927

117807

About the Author

Dale Ralph Davis is pastor of Woodland Presbyterian Church, Hattiesburg, Mississippi. Previously he taught Old Testament at Reformed Theological Seminary, Jackson Mississippi. He has previously written Focus on the Bible commentaries on:

Joshua (978-1-84550-137-2)
Judges(978-1-84550-138-9)
1 Samuel(978-1-85792-516-6)
2 Samuel(978-1-84550-270-6)
1 Kings(978-1-84550-251-5)
2 Kings(978-1-84550-096-2).

PREFACE

This book was not my idea. I'm leery of saying too much about preaching. Over a decade ago I taught a course on expository preaching and concluded from that experience that I never wanted to teach preaching. These pages therefore focus on the proper interpretation of Old Testament narratives in preparation for preaching. A step removed!

I am a bit puzzled over why many Christians seem to think the Old Testament is such a 'problem.' I know the usual answers to that, but I can find many of the same 'difficulties' with the New Testament. I am not so puzzled about why some pastors and teachers are perplexed about expounding Old Testament texts. For nearly two hundred years a skeptical brand of Old Testament criticism has largely held sway in our universities and divinity halls; it 'un-godded' the Old Testament, implied the Old Testament documents were extremely complex and involved, and managed to make Old Testament studies mostly boring, lifeless, and dull. Of course the occasional student finds this high priestly craft of Old Testament criticism attractive. But many simply write the Old Testament off. If it's as complicated as they have been taught, it is far too bewildering and esoteric for them to bother about, except for dipping into the Psalms for occasional funerals.

Examples of this deadening approach literally drip out of commentaries. Look up Exodus 19:21-25 in Martin Noth's *Exodus*. He spends eight lines on the passage, dubs it 'secondary,' makes a couple of factual observations, notes a difficulty on one half verse, and calls the last verse a 'fragment.' Even a passing but half-thoughtful glance at the passage shows a marvelous theology of Yahweh's compassion-in-severity. But Noth can't see it – he's too busy analyzing for fragments and additions.

I'm not on a crusade against the villains of Old Testament studies. One learns even from the 'villains.' And there have been far more hopeful signs in Old Testament studies in recent years. But I still believe that traditional Old Testament criticism has had the effect of killing the Old Testament for the church. This little tome can hardly reverse that, but it is meant as an exercise in reading the Old Testament for fun and profit. As my mother-in-law used to say, 'It's different anyway.' And maybe it will help.

Most of what I do in the following pages involves discussing examples of Old Testament narratives. I have tried to select examples from a broad range of possibilities. I have previously written expository commentaries on Joshua through 2 Kings (available through Christian Focus), but I have tried to cite a majority of my examples outside of those books (to avoid repetition from those commentaries). However, the Joshua-through-2 Kings segment does contain a pile of narrative and so I have had to dip into those materials occasionally. By the way, I assume that you have the biblical text handy in order to carry on your 'Berean' work.

One always owes a debt to his taskmasters! Because of kind invitations in recent years I have been forced to pull together some work on Old Testament narrative. Hence my hearty thanks to hosts and hearers at Proclamation Trust, London; Parkside Church, Chagrin Falls, Ohio; the Scottish Ministry Assembly, Glasgow; Faith Mission Bible College, Edinburgh; *Preaching and Preachers*, South Africa; ministers' fraternals in south Wales; and Reformed Theological Seminary, my erstwhile employer, where I was able to teach courses on Old Testament narrative.

I send forth this study as a token of gratitude to Dr. Alec Motyer, who has always demonstrated that rigorous study and devotional warmth are amicable bedfellows.

Easter 2006, The Resurrection of our Lord

CHAPTER 1

Approach

Begging – the place to start

I was reading Richard Pratt's fine book, *He Gave Us Stories*.
He was discussing what precious little attention we give to the
work of the Holy Spirit in the task of interpreting Scripture.
Of course, some articles and brief pieces discuss this, but
Dr. Pratt stated that to his knowledge the most recent work
of any size on this matter was written by John Owen over
three hundred years ago. I looked up the end note for the
documentation; there Pratt cites Owen and John Owen's
words smacked me between the eyes:

> For a man solemnly to undertake the interpretation of any
> portion of Scripture without invocation of God, to be taught
> and instructed by his Spirit, is a high provocation of him; nor
> shall I expect the discovery of truth from any one who thus
> proudly engages in a work so much above his ability.[1]

We are guilty of arrogance, not merely neglect, when we fail
to beg for the Spirit's help in the study of Scripture. We may
even have such arrogance even when we seem to be seeking
the Spirit's aid – I think of those times when in a light-headed
tokenism we utter our slap-happy prayer that the Lord would
'guide and direct us as we study this passage.' One shudders
to think how flippant we are. But how many more times we
neglect any overt seeking of the Spirit's help! The pressure

is on. The passage must be studied for the sermon or lesson. We pull out our exegetical notes; we grab several of the better commentaries off the shelf; make sure one Bible dictionary of choice is close at hand. Deep into our study time the thought occurs to us that we have not looked – nor did we think of looking – to the God who breathed out this Scripture to give us an understanding of the Scripture. He will likely give that understanding through the tools we use, but when we use tools while neglecting him the tools have become idols.

We may have a high view of the Bible; we may be distraught because large sectors of the church seem to ignore its authority. Yet in our own Scripture work we easily ignore its chief Interpreter. Professionalism rather than piety drives us. We needn't be surprised at our sterility and poverty if we refuse to be beggars for the Spirit's help.

There is that well-worn story of George Gillespie at the meeting of Parliament and the Westminster Assembly. Someone made a long and studious argument in favor of Erastianism.[2] His associates urged young Gillespie to answer it. Gillespie repeated the substance of the previous discourse and refuted it. It was common in the Assembly for those listening to take notes while someone was speaking – as an aid to their own memory. George Gillespie had seemed to be doing just that while listening to the speaker he later refuted. But when his friends could sneak a look at Gillespie's notebook, all they could find were scribblings like, 'Lord, send light,' 'Lord, give assistance,' 'Lord, defend thine own cause.'[3] That must ever be our attitude toward interpreting Scripture. We must begin with the Spirit (cf. Gal. 3:3), and we must not only begin with him but we must keep returning to him again and again. We always must begin with begging.

The Smoke-filled Room and Asking Questions

I think sometimes we can have – or give – the impression that there is a smoke-filled room hidden away somewhere in the Palace of Biblical Interpretation where a few hermeneutical

high priests parcel out the secrets for *really* understanding
Scripture, especially the Old Testament. Of course, this
is simply mental mythology and sometimes it helps for
someone to say so. Hence I was much heartened to read Alec
Moyter's confession:

> There is no special mystique or approach to preaching that
> has to descend on preachers when the Lord leads them to
> minister from the Old rather than from the New. There are
> no special avenues into preaching from the Old Testament
> nor any special tricks of the trade that I can share with you.[4]

Nor do I have any tricks. I cannot offer any magical procedure
which, if followed, will unlock the riches of Old Testament
narrative. I only intend to highlight various angles on
narrative texts which assist in interpretation for preaching
and teaching. I'll cite a bunch of examples which are either
culled from my own study or hawked gratefully – and with
credit – from others. I simply want to stir up the biblical
juices of preachers and students, to help people walk away
from the text muttering about what a delightful book God
has given us. So if you are looking for a learned and intricate
discussion on the aspects of Old Testament narrative or for
a careful and complicated technique for unlocking narrative
texts, you have blundered into the wrong book. Check the
refund policy.

If I reject some esoteric technique that does not mean
I have no procedure or plan when approaching a biblical text.
In facing Scripture one must take account of two realities:
Spirit and text. This fact forces me to one of my operating
presuppositions: *God has given his word in the form of
literature, part of which is narrative; I should therefore use
all available tools for understanding such literature.* So I seek
the Spirit's aid and use an approach suited to the form of his
word. Hence, at the very least, I ask *questions* of the text. This
is my 'procedure' so far as it goes. There is nothing super-

charged about it. I do not follow this regime of questions in any decreed order. It is all very basic. I use it partly because it *is* simple and I can carry it around in my mental hip pocket. Let me briefly discuss these questions.

Why? (Intention). Why did the writer include this text? What was he trying to get across by relating it? What does he mean to teach by/in it? It's safe to say that usually the writer's purpose is *theocentric* – he intends to communicate something about God, i.e., his character, purposes, demands, or ways. Sometimes intention is obvious, right on the surface of the text. Note 1 Kings 12:15 and 24 for understanding Rehoboam's fiasco. And if one pays attention to Yahweh's statement in Judges 7:2 it will keep one from accusing most of Gideon's men of drinking in a 'self-centred manner' (a la one expositor). At other times repetition may betray intention (see Gen. 39, Exod. 1, and 2 Kings 1). Sometimes the literary shape of the passage helps isolate the intention (e.g., Rahab's confession of faith at the heart of Joshua 2, or the Spirit's power at the hinge of 1 Sam. 11:1-11). Or the writer may suck you into his intention by drawing you into the particular mood of the story (try 2 Sam. 13). Again, it may be the strange stuff that leads you to his intention – Why, for example, a genealogy as the climax of the Book of Ruth (Ruth 4:18-22)?

Of course, the skeptic is perfectly free to ask whether we can always be sure we have – or can get at – the writer's intention. Maybe not, but I find that stubbornly asking this question opens up more texts for me. What is this doing here? Why on earth would anyone tell this strange story at this point? It is good exercise in itself and, more often than not, it yields pay dirt. If one still comes up empty, Walter Kaiser's counsel shows the 'way of escape': '[W]henever we are at a loss as to what we should preach on a passage, *we will never go wrong if we focus on God*, his actions and his requirements.'[5]

Now all this concern with a writer's intention is terribly out of step. I call it 'dinosaur hermeneutics.' Reader-response criticism is more the current rage; it only wants to answer, 'How does this text affect me?' There is no precise or correct meaning but only meanings which arise from within the reader.[6] I admit my preoccupation with a writer's intention is dated. And I really don't care. It's hard to get away from the suspicion that someone meant to mean something with a text. Sooner or later folks will recognize that – again.

Where? (Context). I have a note from our middle son when he was in middle school. It's on a torn-off slip of paper and reads: 'Wake me up at 7:30 tomorrow morning so I can read the Bible.' You might think we raised a very pious thirteen-year-old. But you have to understand the 'context': our boys were avid fans and imitators of those muscular dramatists of 'professional wrestling.' They would watch it on TV and then put on their own shows. Because of the time they spent watching this stuff, I, instead of forbidding it, legislated that they had to do an hour of Bible reading for every hour they were going to watch wrestling. My parental wisdom or lack thereof is not the issue here. The point is that knowing the context may temper your estimate of Seth's piety.

And so of every text or narrative we always ask: Where does this occur? Where does it occur literarily? What story comes before it? What account follows it? Does remembering Genesis 27, for example, affect the way you hear Genesis 28:13-15? Where does the text appear historically? The Book of Lamentations is not a narrative text, but who would dream of interpreting the 'great is thy faithfulness' of chapter 3 apart from the smoke, ruin, and despair of 587 BC? Or where does the text occur religiously or culturally? Knowing something about paganism, for example, helps one with 1 Kings 18:27 (and Ps. 121:3-4).

How? (Structure). I want to know if the text is 'packaged' in a certain way. Does it have a symmetrical development? Is it put together after a definite pattern? Does the structure reveal an intended emphasis (cf. my remarks on 'intention')? I also include in this category matters of literary art. Simply recognizing the intended contrast between the captive Israelite girl and the unbelieving Israelite king in 2 Kings 5:2-7 can't but stir homiletic juices.

What? (Content). Much of the grunt work of exposition happens here. We must carefully observe what is in the text. I especially focus on what may be puzzling – it may be a word or phrase or idea which I feel I must understand in order to grasp the passage properly. I want to isolate the conundrums that keep me from understanding the text – and solve as many as possible. But much of my time in this category may simply consist of close observation of the text. And there may not be a whole slug of problems. I may simply need to observe, ponder, and draw inferences. Think of Jonah 1:1-2:

> Now the word of Yahweh came to Jonah son of Amittai, saying: 'Rise, go to Nineveh, that great city, and preach against it, for their evil has come up before me.'

Simply *thinking* about the text shows there are at least two implications in it – or two assumptions Yahweh makes: (1) Every nation is accountable to him. Yahweh may be specially the God of Israel but he assumes pagan nations (like Assyria) are accountable to him. He is a 'world-class' deity, not the mascot of an Israelite ghetto. (2) Every servant owes obedience to him. He assumes he has the right to command the obedience of specific human servants. So in two verses one sees Yahweh's sovereignty depicted in the big sweep and in the personal dimension. Here is, in the same text, both international and individual sovereignty. God makes the most massive assumptions. This comes from simple observation of the text.

So what? (Appropriation/Application). There's a story in American baseball lore about Lou Novikoff ('The Mad Russian'), who was an outfielder for the Chicago Cubs. Like many baseball players he was superstitious – he insisted that his wife Esther deride him from the stands. He claimed her mockery inspired him. It all began when Novikoff was playing in the Pacific Coast League. He stepped up to bat. Esther was in a box seat behind home plate, and she yelled, 'You big bum! You can't hit!' Lou swung on the first pitch and smacked it over the left-field wall for a home run. Fans asked Esther why she berated her husband like that. She patiently explained that she did it to make him mad because 'when he gets mad, he gets hits.' Novikoff had a fine year and then went up to the Chicago Cubs for the 1941 season. He had to leave his family behind and he turned in a poor showing that year. But at the 1942 season opener when Novikoff stepped to the plate, a female voice rang out from the box seats: 'Strike the big bum out! He can't hit!' It was his loving Esther. Novikoff smacked a base hit.[7]

Now biblical interpretation is a bit like that. We need to hear some loving mockery behind us, crying, 'So what? What difference does all this study make for anyone? Why should I want to pay any attention to this?' If we are constantly 'berated' that way, it will make us far better interpreters.

More on this later. In my view, however, if we omit 'application,' if we fail to answer the 'So what?', we are short-circuiting the whole purpose of Scripture ('and is profitable for...,' 2 Tim. 3:16). If I cannot rub the results of my labor into the pores of the souls of God's people (or of pagans), why am I taking the trouble to do this? If what I study won't preach, there is something wrong with the way I study what I study.

Those are my questions. There's no reek of the smoke-filled room on them. And remember: they are no sure-fire formula. We only hope they will be tools the Spirit will use.

In the e.g. mode...

Look at Judges 13. We can use it as an example of how these questions press us into the text – and then from the text. We're not looking at all the details of the chapter, only some highlights for illustration.

Notice verses 2-5. Here we meet inability, obscurity, and promise. That's a matter of content – the 'what?' question. This woman is both barren (like Sarah in Gen. 11:30) and nameless. She is simply Manoah's wife – she has no name. The memory of Sarah's situation (and that of other biblical 'barrens') can help you here. Isn't this all vintage Yahweh? Starting with nothing, with helplessness, with people who don't have the power even for natural work? And isn't it like him to choose obscure folks as servants? He has no bias for bluebloods. Have we not passed out of 'what?' into 'so what?'?

We also find a clear clue about the 'why?', the intention of the writer. Well, at least we have Yahweh's intention clearly stated in giving a son to Mrs. Manoah: 'And he will begin to save Israel from the grip of the Philistines' (v. 5b). Apparently the writer's purpose is to tell us how Yahweh raised up this savior who would begin to save. But we have run into other saviors God has raised up in this book and so this story of a coming savior invites comparison with the previous ones. To some degree this raises the 'how?' question, not in terms of the literary structure of Judges 13 but of the literary contrast between this savior story and all the preceding ones in the book. This Samson will be different from other judges in Judges, for here God isn't using someone who's already on the scene knocking around the hill country of Ephraim somewhere. No, here we have a nativity story – the only one in Judges. God will *grow* a deliverer this time. God is not in a hurry. Indeed, according to verse 5, Samson will only 'begin to save.' Deliverance will be a long haul. Yahweh has a plan but he is not in a panic.

Doesn't this literary observation with its theological freight spill over into the 'so what?' category? Doesn't this come home for you? Doesn't God's deliberate pace bother you sometimes? You set deadlines and he ignores them. There's a deliverance you need, a trial that seems excruciating, and he has not rushed to put everything to rights. Does this text then solve your dilemma? No. But it at least tells you that you are likely dealing with the real God, for, according to the Scripture, you are facing one of his typical ways.

When I was in high school the teen-age fellows in our congregation took up the offering at our church's morning worship service. For whatever reason, the church leaders had given the oversight of this task to one of our friends, Dennis. That was no problem, except that an unbiased observer could tell that the 'authority' of the position had gone to Dennis' head and made him a bit pompous. One Sunday morning we were singing the hymn before the offering. My friend Dave and I were in a sort of overflow alcove. For some reason Dave had an anxiety attack. He nudged me and indicated that Dennis must have forgotten about having ushers down for the offering. It was nearing the end of the hymn and no ushers were coming down when they should. Why I didn't use my sense and tell Dave to allow Dennis to dangle in his own swagger, I'll never know. So, quick and efficient young fellows that we were, Dave, myself, and two other lads walked in from the side and piously took our position in front of the communion table to await the offertory prayer. Of course, the hymn was not *quite* over and momentarily one felt the tremor in the floor as Dennis and his own legion of ushers began coming down the aisle from the rear of the sanctuary. Fortunately, there was another side door to the left of us that led into the church parking lot, and we usurping ushers quickly vacated and dashed through it. It was both embarrassing and stupid; it came from that impulse that can't wait. And we really run into problems when we think Yahweh should have high blood pressure like we do. It's a whole lesson, isn't it, in the usual ways of God?

That is not a full look at Judges 13. But the passage easily shows that God is surprising (vv. 1-5), fearful (see vv. 8-23), and deliberate (vv. 5, 24-25). And whenever you see God clearly in a text you can be sure there is something very applicable there for you.

Endnotes

1. Cited in Richard L. Pratt, Jr., *He Gave Us Stories* (Brentwood, TN: Wolgemuth & Hyatt, 1990), 404.

2. The view that the state has the right to intervene and overrule in church affairs.

3. James Reid, *Memoirs of the Westminster Divines* (1811; reprint ed., Edinburgh: Banner of Truth, 1982), 2:281-82.

4. Alec Motyer, 'Preaching from the Old Testament,' in *Preaching the Living Word* (Ross-shire: Christian Focus, 1999), 99.

5. Walter C. Kaiser, Jr., *Preaching and Teaching from the Old Testament* (Grand Rapids: Baker, 2003), 57 (emphasis mine).

6. Dan McCartney and Charles Clayton, *Let the Reader Understand* (Wheaton: Bridgepoint, 1994), 281. See their discussion and cf. also Walter C. Kaiser, Jr., and Moises Silva, *An Introduction to Biblical Hermeneutics* (Grand Rapids: Zondervan, 1994), 240-45 (by Silva). A reader should be appropriating a text's meaning – but not determining it.

7. Bruce Nash and Allan Zullo, *The Baseball Hall of Shame 4* (New York: Pocket Books, 1990), 180.

CHAPTER 2

Quirks

I have a small, red, Ford pick-up truck that serves as my main transportation. It has its peculiarities. There have been times when I could push in the clutch, turn the key, and nothing would happen. However, if I would then let out the clutch, depress it again, and turn the key, it would start. This did not happen at every attempted start – only occasionally. More recently it seems to have gotten 'healed,' for it hasn't done this for some time now. Or there was the day I was taking one of our members to the airport to catch a flight to Virginia. He happened to glance at the fuel gauge, saw it was on empty, and quickly suggested I might want to get gasoline since the airport was sixty miles away. I calmly informed him that the gauge did not work and that I could tell the approximate amount of gas I had from my odometer reading. After all, repairing a fuel gauge runs into triple figures and I can do math cheaper than that. All of which is to say that there are some quirks my pick-up has and anyone who operates it does well to know about them.

The same goes for biblical narrative. Narrative has some of its own peculiarities and anyone interpreting it should be alert to these. They are, I suppose, a pretty basic bunch of characteristics, but we should be on the lookout for them. Most all of them fall into the category of literary features we need to recognize. I'll highlight a few of them and try to indicate how noting literary quirks can sometimes lead to homiletical pay-dirt.

Reticence

We want, when reading narrative, to get into the narrator's own head, to know how he looks upon the matters he describes, or – what is the same for me, how God looks upon those matters. Sometimes a writer makes his point of view unmissable. For example, all through 2 Samuel 11 the writer portrays David's affair with Bathsheba all the way from lust to cover-up with no overt assessment from his pen. Nor does he insert marginal comments like 'Gasp here!' or 'Sigh sadly' along the way. He is almost clinical in the way he depicts David's fall; but in the very last line of the chapter he leaves no doubt: what David had done was evil in Yahweh's eyes (v. 27b).

The problem is that writers don't always include revealing last lines. As Kaiser points out, 'Rarely does the author of a [narrative] text state what the point of the story is; that is left to interpretation.'[1] Old Testament narratives are often mute when it comes to 'point of view.' We are meant to 'divine' that. Check 1 Samuel 27, David's Ziklag days. There is no mention or allusion to God at all. How does Yahweh or the writer look upon David's desperate flight to Philistia and his conduct while there? There are no overt theological clues. Or take Genesis 37. Most of us probably come to it with a Joseph-bias. And certainly one cannot miss the hatred of his brothers nor the fact that only filthy lucre kept them from filthy murder. And yet the whole chapter is all description. God is not mentioned. Strictly speaking, we are not told what he is doing in this episode nor what he thinks of all of it. Are we, for example, to take Joseph's telling of his dreams as perfectly proper or as a bit of teenage one-up-man-ship designed to dig his brothers?

No need to go into despair over narrative's occasional reserve. But like most quirks we should make note of it. And biblical writers probably have a reason behind this reserve: they probably want us to *think* about their stories. Why should they always spoon-feed us?

Eavesdropping

STP Oil Treatment (the motor oil additive) used to advertise that said product gave common motorists 'the racer's edge.' Biblical narrators often give us what I call 'the reader's edge,' that is, they inform us of something before the characters in the story know of it. As readers we get to eavesdrop behind the scenes of the story. For example, in Joshua 9 we know about the Gibeonites' deception (vv. 3-5) a good while before Joshua and Israel face it. We may frequently know things the biblical characters don't, and sometimes this fact is crucial for interpretation.

It certainly is in the book of Job. Job 1:6-12 and 2:1-7a give you the reader's edge. You get to eavesdrop behind the scenes. But look at Job's story from Job's sandals. That means you know *nothing* of what has gone on in those exchanges in 1:6-12 and 2:1-7a. *For Job* the story goes from sacrifice and prayer for his children (1:5) to the Sabeans attacking and pilfering his oxen and donkeys (1:13ff.). After his possessions are ravaged, his servants slain, and his family perishes, Job worships (1:20-21); 'Yahweh has given and Yahweh has taken away.' The next thing Job knows gross sores break out all over his body (2:7b). Job has no clue about the momentous issues at stake in 1:6-12 and 2:1-7a because he knows none of that. As the reader you know, but Job does not. This 'ignorance' is not something Job is to be blamed for. But this whole story can be deceptive for you (and unfair to Job) unless you realize that you possess data Job never has. He has neither videos nor tapes of those exchanges between Yahweh and the adversary. He *goes through his whole struggle in the dark*, knowing nothing of the accuser who ridicules his loyalty nor of the fact that Yahweh has steadfastly been for him.

Does not this simple observation point to a useful application?[2] Frequently we do not have nearly enough information to form a correct estimate of our trials. We must remember how much we do not know.

In October 1940 a fellow came from Spain to Britain who allegedly wanted to study the British Boy Scouts during wartime. The Brits knew he was a spy in the pay of Berlin but let him see plenty of Boy Scouts while they stage-managed other displays. One of their brightest ploys occurred when they took him to Scotland by plane. Britain's air power was very thin at the time – a few Hurricanes and fewer Spitfires. But all the way to Scotland they ran into squadron upon squadron of Spitfires. The sky was glutted with them. Of course, the spy didn't know it was the same squadron diving in and out of the clouds and coming over and over again from all angles and altitudes. The same thing took place on the way back to London – hundreds of Spitfires. The agent's report went off to Berlin – Britain was an armed camp.[3] He didn't have a clue because he had no idea of what was being done (for him) behind the scenes.

That is the situation in Job. There is so much we do not see. There may be far more going on than we know. We must let that temper our exasperation and discouragement in our trials. And getting at this begins with simply a literary observation.

Selectivity

Here we are concerned with what a writer includes and what he omits, with what he tells us and what he does not tell us. One must assume that he wants to tell us what he tells us and that what he does not tell us is – in his view and for some reason – not necessary.

You can get a taste of a writer's selectivity in 1 Kings 13. Read through the chapter, noting what the writer tells you and what he does *not* tell you but which you are dying to know. You have scads of questions. Why did the old prophet lie to the man of God from Judah? How could a liar then speak a true prophecy? Why was this old prophet so weird? You are dying of curiosity and the narrator answers none of your questions. Hence they must not be that important!

One must assume then that a writer includes what he thinks important and omits what is irrelevant. Perhaps this explains Genesis 22:3? We are told of Abraham's obedience but not of his feelings (except indirectly). Is that significant? What are we to make of the fact that the writer of Jonah does not tidy up the end of the book and tell us how Jonah responded to Yahweh's closing statement and final question (Jonah 4:10-11)? Is that in one sense irrelevant? Is he trying to suck us into facing that question rather than relating the facts about Jonah? (Note Luke's omission of how Simon's case turned out after Acts 8:24).[4]

Sometimes a writer will draw attention to his method, as if to say, 'N.b., I'm being selective!' A classic and instructive example of this occurs in Genesis 16 and 17 in the Abraham cycle. In 16:16 we are told that Abram was 86 years old when Ishmael was born. Then in 17:1, the very next verse, we read: 'When Abram was 99 years old, Yahweh appeared to Abram...' There's a chronological gap of 13 years that falls through the crack between these two chapters. So the writer is saying as kindly as he can, 'I am not giving you an exhaustive biography of Abraham; I am giving you premier moments in Abraham's life.' So we get to the end of Genesis 16, we blink, and find ourselves 13 years down the time-line in 17:1. But the writer is not being deceptive. He tells us straight out what he's doing.

He is not only being very selective but very helpful as well, for by his careful 'time notes' he not only alerts us to the fact of his selectivity but instructs us in the troubles of faith. There are 13 years of which we know nothing. Add to that the 10 years of 16:3 (cf. 12:4). That's a long time and still no seed and no son as Yahweh had promised (12:7 and 15:4). So by dropping 13 years into the dumpster of history between

chapters 16 and 17 the writer underscores the struggle of
Abraham's faith. What happened in those 13 years? Oh, what
had happened during the previous decade-plus. Abraham
played veterinarian to his goats, settled scraps among his
herdsmen, sat up with Sarah when she had the flu, sent scouts
out to look for water sources for the flocks – in short, all the
sorts of things that one does in the wash-your-face, brush-
your-teeth, go-to-work routine of daily living. And year
follows year that way, and Yahweh's promise goes unfulfilled.
Is the writer not telling us that *time* can be a severe problem
for faith? That it can be hard to go on believing when you
have to walk on in ordinary, run-of-the-mill living without
seeing any of the fireworks of promise?

Sarcasm

Occasionally the biblical writer dips his pen in acid and uses
mockery, derision, or put-down to drive home his point. The
device may not be prevalent but likely occurs more often
than a casual reader thinks.

One thinks immediately, of course, of Elijah's taunting
the prophets of Baal on Mt. Carmel in 1 Kings 18:27. Elijah
alleges that Baal may be preoccupied with a plethora of
'divine' activities like travel, napping, or using the facilities.
But one finds such ridicule elsewhere, if perhaps less
blatantly. One overhears it when Laban accuses Jacob of
stealing his household deities: 'But why did you steal my
gods?' (Gen. 31:30). Any full-blooded Yahweh-worshiping
hearer/reader would think, 'My, what sort of gods are those
that can't keep from being pilfered?' And anyone who is
possessed both with orthodoxy and a sense of humor (too
often a rare combination) laughs when these deities 'feel'
both Rachel's warmth and weight while she is 'indisposed'
(31:34-35). The same ridicule seeps out of Micah's helpless
rage toward the Danites in Judges 18:24: 'You take my gods
that I made and the priest, and go away, and what have I left?'
(ESV). What indeed! And, of course, the biblical writer is at

his nasty best when describing the divine 'trauma' of Dagon before the ark of Yahweh in 1 Samuel 5:1-5; not only do the Philistines have to pick Dagon up but would've been most happy with an ample supply of super-glue. One even hears a hint of mockery in the common but repeated 'made' in 1 Kings 12:28-33 (Jeroboam's cult) and in 2 Kings 17:29-31 (imported pagans in the land of Israel). Note too the helplessness of pagan resources in Genesis 41:8, 24, and in Daniel 1:20; 2:1-11; 4:6-7, 18; 5:8, 15, all of which smells like devout scoffing – because those helpless resources are the foil for the true God's provision via Joseph and Daniel.

One of the most subtle but powerful samples of sarcasm comes in Daniel 3. Here all of Nebuchadnezzar's civil service corps is to observe the required moment of silence before his 90 by 9 feet image. It's likely a government-sponsored loyalty exercise; devotees can naturally go back to their private superstitions and 'personal faith'; they simply need to worship here if they want to keep their jobs – and their lives. The pressure is powerful; after all, it's the law. And when all the satraps and postal workers have their back sides in the air and their noses in the sand before Nebuchadnezzar's giant dummy on the Plain of Dura, well, it's hard to resist. The 'church music' alone is impressive (vv. 4-5, 7, 10, 15). And yet the writer both tells the story and mocks the 'worship.' He both reports and ridicules at the same time. At least I think so. He repeatedly uses the verb 'set up' (Aram. *qum*) as he refers to Nebuchadnezzar's image, nine times to be exact (vv. 1, 2, 3 [twice], 5, 7, 12, 14, 18); one can also throw in 'made' twice, vv. 1, 15). Perhaps I'm seeing things, but highlight the usages of 'set up' in your text, read it over noting them, and it all seems to have a cumulative impact. It's a 'set-up job,' as we say. It's as if the writer is saying, 'It may seem fearful (because it has all the muscle of the government behind it), but it's a farce! If you can see behind the mask, if you can see the falsehood and stupidity of it all, if you can hear heaven's laughter over it [Ps. 2:4], you need not be taken in by it. True, the furnace is hot but the image is just hot air. It's simply a little posturing by a human king strutting around in his big international pants' (cf. Isa. 46:7).

Sarcasm is a form of humor. And I have observed that whenever Scripture is delightfully humorous it is also deadly serious. There is always a serious point being made when the biblical writer uses humor. Hence we should keep our ears tuned for sarcasm.

Imagination

We are accustomed to poetic and/or prophetic texts that appeal to imagination. When, for example, David wanted to tell how Yahweh had intervened in answer to his prayer, it took him nine verses and nearly upsetting the universe to tell of it (Ps. 18:7-15). And Nahum takes you through flashing storms, empty oceans, trembling mountains, and a wasted world to impress you with Yahweh's majesty (Nahum 1:3b-5) because he wants you to *tremble* before his majesty and be utterly convinced of his ability to avenge evil and put all to rights (1:2-3, 6). Some Bible readers may wonder why David couldn't simply say 'God answers prayers,' or why Nahum couldn't be content with 'the Lord is majestic.' Why do they have to go on and on and take us through the universe and back? Because they not only want to *inform* you of God's might and majesty but *impress* you with his might and majesty – and they likely know that to do that they need to give you not only facts for your brain but pictures for your imagination.

But narrative texts can also make use of imagination. Biblical narrators have no video and so must get you to see or feel matters through the written word ('verbeo,' I suppose). Take a look at Joshua 11:1-5. It's a description of the Jabin-led northern coalition that gathered to oppose Joshua and Israel. But why does the writer heap up this mass of royalty (vv. 1-2a), geography (v. 2b), ethnicity (v. 3), and hyperbole (v. 4)? Instead of these five verses why don't we have a brief, concise summary like, 'Jabin assembled a humongous army in order to assault Israel'? Ten words would have done it. Why does the writer use 71 Hebrew words or 153 English words (NASB) and drag you all over northern Palestine before he allows you to breathe?

Perhaps football can help us. Now I cannot re-create on paper the sense of rivalry that exists in the Southeastern Conference of American college football. But suffice it to say that only a few years ago Mississippi State won, unbelievably, over Auburn by a score of 18-16. Let's say you heard neither the game nor the score. So a day or two later you ask some State fans about the game. Would they say, 'State won 18-16'? Could you get them to say that? No. Would they listen to your protest if you said, 'Hey, I don't want the play-by-play – just give me the score'? They would retort, 'You can't understand, you can't appreciate the game with only the score; see, you have to understand what State was facing. They were down 16-3, with a little over two minutes left in the game, and then...' Then they would go on with the miraculous and minute events of those two-minutes-plus. Only then would you be properly impressed.

So with the biblical writers. They didn't have camcorders; they had to put it all into words. And sometimes they multiply words and deluge you with words so that you will get the true picture. As in Joshua 11:1-5. Line upon line, detail upon detail, danger upon danger, enemy upon enemy finally batter you into seeing what an absolutely hopeless situation Israel faces and how impossible Yahweh's salvation frequently looks.[5]

Surprise

Biblical narrative is laced with 'shockers,' whether major or minor. Sometimes we may be so familiar with the flow of a biblical story that we fail to be surprised when we should. We need to cultivate a 'first-time-reader' frame of mind. Usually biblical surprises prove instructive.

The Book of Jonah slaps us with a surprise with scarcely a chance to warm up. We read that the 'word of Yahweh came' to Jonah, that he was to get up, go to Nineveh and preach against it, and then: 'Jonah rose up to flee to Tarshish from the presence of Yahweh – he went down to Joppa...' (Jonah 1:3).[6] Now prophets have all sorts of reactions when they are called – they are devastated (Isa. 6:5), intimidated (Jer. 1:6-8), angry and bitter (Ezek. 3:14-15). But only Jonah has the gall to say, 'I'm outta here!'

Of course, Yahweh is not passive: 'But *Yahweh* [emphatic] hurled a great wind on the sea' (1:4). Jonah disobeys and God starts throwing things! But the surprises continue. The ship looks destined to smash up, the sailors are scared out of their wits, 'but Jonah had gone down below deck, had lain down, and was sound asleep' (1:5). Kind of disposes of the myth of the tortured conscience, doesn't it? Perhaps we've heard someone warning that one can turn one's back on God's call but 'you'll never have peace about it.' Didn't seem to affect Jonah's sleep. It's not like Jonah's overdosing on antacids or guzzling Milk of Magnesia. He seems to have perfect peace about running away from God's call. Sometimes, to be sure, one of the Lord's fleeing servants may be in great turmoil over such disobedience. But not necessarily, not always. Have you ever had a church member who's leaving his wife for another woman tell you that he's having some of the best 'quiet times' he's ever had? I have. Blatant disobedience and subjective peace can bed down together. What does such peace mean? Nothing. Feelings are only feelings. Jonah's peace is no accurate indicator of the true state of affairs. That can be a bit scary. And it all begins with a surprise.

One meets another one in Joshua 5. As soon as Yahweh brings Israel through the Jordan into Canaan he commands Joshua to circumcise a generation of men (Josh. 5:2-3) who formed the cream of Israel's army (5:5). A bit of heaven's gall, it seems, even if the enemy is intimidated (5:1). Anyone with a bit of a memory knows what can happen to a people whose fighting men have been rendered helpless during recovery from such surgery (see Gen. 34:25-29). Yet here in hostile territory Yahweh first off requires Joshua to disable his whole army. But the 'insane' procedure packs its own point: Israel's protection rests with the arm of Yahweh not with the sword of her warriors, and, even more, covenant fidelity (expressed in the covenant sign of circumcision) is always more urgent than military preparedness; in a word, holiness trumps pragmatism in Yahweh's order.

That is one of the functions of biblical surprises – to indicate some urgency. Something like the time when folks at New Park Street Chapel discovered that the windows in the upper balcony had been smashed out. Obviously the work of some vandal. Actually, the pastor, Charles Spurgeon, had several times asked the Deacons to open up permanently some of those windows. The building was low-lying, hemmed in, and insufferably hot and stuffy. Maybe that's what gave the Deacons inertia! In any case, nothing was done – until the night when the benevolent crime took place. There may well have been nicks, scratches, and glass fragments on Spurgeon's cane, however, for he later confessed to some of his students that 'I have walked with the stick which let the oxygen into that stifling structure.'[7] Behind the shock there was a certain urgency – in Spurgeon's case, for ventilation; in Joshua 5, for consecration.

While we are in Joshua note the water-in-the-face effect of Joshua 24:19. Joshua had been evangelizing Israel, pressing them to be certain to 'serve' Yahweh (the verb occurs 14 times in Joshia 24:14-24). He is calling them to first-commandment loyalty (Exod. 20:3). Joshua comes down with his 'as-for-me-and-my-house' resolution to serve Yahweh (vv. 14-15) and then Israel declares her similar resolve (vv. 16-18). And Joshua will have none of it!

> You are not able to serve Yahweh, for he is a holy God, he is a jealous God; he will not forgive your rebellion and your sins (v. 19).

Imagine Joshua conducting an evangelistic rally. He makes his plea, presses home his call. The music starts. People begin to come forward. And Joshua rushes out, grabs the microphone, and cries, 'No! No! You don't understand. Get back to your seats. Better yet, go home – you really need to think this over.' Joshua, of course, is not trying to turn people away from Yahweh but to keep them from blandly coming to him, from one of those of-course-this-is-what-we-should-do commitments. Israel must understand that Yahweh is not craving their attention but searching their earnestness. When they come to Yahweh they will meet red-hot holiness rather than gushing acceptance. They must know the sort of God they are claiming to serve. Verse 19 would serve as a splendid antidote to some contemporary 'evangelism.'

Surprises in Scripture usually conceal vital preaching points, which is why preachers should always keep their eyes peeled for biblical shocks.

Emphasis (Repetition)

Biblical writers did not have the luxury of using bold, italicized, or underlined type as our computer-driven generation does. They had to make their emphases in different ways. Repetition was one means they used as a substitute for underscoring. Since this matter will arise again (chapter 9), let me simply touch on one passage as an example–Daniel 1.

One bumps into three 'theological' statements in Daniel 1, each one using the verb 'gave':

> And the Lord gave Jehoiakim king of Judah into his [Nebuchadnezzar's] hand, with some of the vessels of the house of God (v. 2).

> And God gave Daniel favor and compassion in the sight of the chief of the eunuchs (v. 9).

> As for these four youths, God gave them learning and skill in all letters and wisdom (v. 17).

God's 'giving' operates in the turn of (what we would call major) historical events (v. 2), in the quirks of personal circumstances (v. 9), and in the success of vocational work (v. 17). Folks in Babylon may be singing, 'Praise Marduk, from whom all blessings flow,' because of Nebuchadnezzar's successful foray against Judah, but our writer knows the real explanation – the Lord 'gave' Jehoiakim up to Nebuchadnezzar (v. 2). We may be tempted to say Daniel got a lucky break with the food service bureaucrats, but the writer corrects such nonsense (v. 9). No doubt those four young fellows studied strenuously for their M. Bab. degree (v. 5b), but their learning and skill were still God's gift (v. 17).

One cannot read Daniel 1 attentively without noticing these three distinct theological notes, these three 'gave' statements. And yet one has to say that in this context the Lord's 'giving' has a subversive or undercover ring to it. The story begins with the dominance of a Babylonian victory and continues under the prevalence of a Babylonian culture – and yet inside all that political power and cultural saturation the God of Israel is quietly, unobtrusively, at work. And we shouldn't miss it.

Donald Grey Barnhouse told of a man who operated an ice house and lost a good watch in the sawdust there. He offered a reward, so men combed the sawdust with rakes, but without success. When the searchers left the building for lunch, a small boy went into the ice house, coming out – a few minutes later – with the watch! Asked how he found it, he simply replied, 'I just lay down in the sawdust and listened. Finally I heard the watch ticking.' That's the way with the Lord's work in Daniel 1 – it's in the quiet mode and we must listen carefully for it. Literarily, the writer's repetition alerts us to it; but experientially, when, like Daniel & Co., we may be pawns of pagan power and swamped with pagan culture, we may well miss it. But what encouragement once we see God's grace hasn't stopped flowing even when we are in Babylon.

Intensity

Here I refer to passages I would call 'concentrated' or 'packed,' where the writer seems to cram so much into a short space in order, I assume, to produce a certain effect on the hearer or reader. Let me trot out several examples.

Joshua 24:1-13 is not necessarily an extremely concise passage. But when you think that Joshua surveys Yahweh's grace to Israel stretching over six hundred years and does it in thirteen verses – well, that's reasonably concentrated. Joshua wants to review the King's grace (vv. 2-13) before he presses the King's demand (vv. 14ff.) upon Israel, and so he packs years of the goodness of Yahweh into these few verses. Elsewhere I have fleshed this out in more detail.[8] Here permit me simply to outline Joshua's overview:

> The surprising grace of God (vv. 2b-3a)
> The gradual pace of God (vv. 3b-4a)
> The mystifying ways of God (v. 4b)
> The manifest power of God (vv. 5-7, 8, 11-12)
> The faithful protection of God (vv. 9-10)
> The continuous provision of God (vv. 7b, 13)

With this God-saturated, grace-soaked review of their history Joshua wants to bring Israel to say, 'O to grace how great a debtor, daily I'm constrained to be!' All of this leads up to his 'therefore' (v. 14). He wants the history of grace to draw his Israel into the fetters of grace: 'Now therefore fear Yahweh and serve him with whole-heartedness and fidelity' (v. 14a). He piles up the reasons and packs the logic into verses 2-13 to make the compulsion of verses 14-15 unavoidable. And why shouldn't the first commandment have first place?

Take a look at Ruth 1:1-5. Right away we meet the big word, 'famine' (v. 1a; quite likely a judgment on Israel at large; cf. Deut. 28:17-18, 38-40, 48); then we hear of the big move (v. 1b; whether justified or not need not concern us here), and then of the bad fact – Elimelech dies (v. 3). So now we have one death, one widow, and two sons (v. 3b). Next we read of two marriages, ten years, two more deaths, and so three total losses (vv. 4-5). You can tally up the mathematics of trouble: one famine, three deaths, three widows, ten years, five verses. That is the opening block of the Book of Ruth. It is sudden and sobering and instructive. Is it not telling us that one's whole life can fall apart in five verses? That such stuff can actually happen to the people of God? Five tightly-packed verses ought to cure us of falling for the 'Prosperity Gospel.'

Take a look at 2 Kings 11:1-3 as well. One humongous emergency of the kingdom of God is stuffed into three verses in the middle of 2 Kings. That wretched swine Athaliah wiped out 'all the royal seed' (v. 1). Well, almost. It looked like she had made mincemeat of Yahweh's Davidic covenant (2 Sam. 7), had driven God's promise into the ground, and left it dead and buried.

> Then Jehosheba, daughter of King Jehoram, sister of Ahaziah, took Joash, Ahaziah's son, and stole him from the midst of the king's sons who were to be massacred – [took] him and his nurse into a room for beds; so they hid him from Athaliah and he was not put to death (v. 2).

Aunt Jehosheba, the godly kidnapper! Who could have known that about 840 BC Yahweh's whole plan of redemption would hang by a single, fragile thread? God's intention to bring his Messiah into the world through David's line will come to nothing if Athaliah makes David's line lineless. But isn't it fascinating how Yahweh always seems to have one of his subversive agents ready to frustrate the designs of the Serpent's cronies? Yahweh's plan of salvation looks so terribly tenuous and open to sabotage, so hand-to-mouth, as it wends its way through history. But he always seems to have an unknown servant in deadly places to foil the enemy. So much catastrophe and rescue, fury and fidelity, are packed into a brief clip of text. And you can preach your whole Advent sermon from three verses.

Tension

It's usually not very tricky to spot tension or suspense in a biblical narrative. If we are alive as we read we can usually detect it! Sometimes one *feels* it before expressly observing it. This may happen at 2 Kings 2:1-6. Elisha tenaciously refuses to leave Elijah's side (vv. 2, 4, 6) and at both Bethel and Jericho the sons of the prophets secretly enlighten Elisha about Elijah's imminent 'home-going' (vv. 3, 5). Elisha, who is no slouch as a prophet himself, tells them to shush, that he already knows. All of a sudden we are breathing the air of suppressed tension – everyone knows of Elijah's departure but no one will talk about it (openly). This tension, of course, sets the stage for the rest of the story.

But often the tension is an integral part of the theology of a narrative text, in which case we dare not stop with literary appreciation but move on to grab hold of the theological significance. Tension texts are often meant to be 'thinkers' on the providence of God.

Who can fail to be in knots by the middle of the Book of Esther? And yet no sooner do we hear that Esther will make her request at her *second* dinner party for the king and Haman than a sub-plot enters the picture that winds the suspense to breaking point. Haman is almost on top of the world; he dines with the king and queen. But as long as Mordecai, that stinking Jew, refuses to pander to him Haman will remain unfulfilled. As he recites his boring resumé to his wife and cronies, he mentions Mordecai as the one blemish on his otherwise perfect life (5:11-13). They advise Haman to build a gallows for Mordecai's immediate future and 'in the morning' to tell the king to have Mordecai hung there. 'On that night the king could not sleep' (6:1). He just happened to have a case of insomnia. He just happened to ask for the chronicles to be brought and read to him (v. 2). It just happened that part of the chronicles selected told of how Mordecai had foiled a plot on the king's life (v. 2; 2:21-23). It just happened that the king was attentive and interested enough to ask how

Mordecai had been honored for his pro-royal deed (v. 3). It so happened that just as the king was meditating on how he must honor Mordecai Haman appeared in the court to speak to the king about hanging Mordecai (v. 4). Well, you know the rest: Haman's plunge to shame, his second banquet, and his own gallows' destiny.

What is important to see, however, is that at the end of Esther 5 Mordecai is a dead duck. Esther (ratcheting up the suspense?) has delayed her request for the rescue of the Jews until her second dinner party (5:8). But after Haman's conference with his 'kitchen cabinet' (5:14), he plans to liquidate Mordecai the next day, in plenty of time to go to Esther's banquet *completely* on top of the world (which means a world minus Mordecai). Esther's orchestrated scheme and surprise revelation may save the Jews but can do nothing for Mordecai. If Mordecai is to be saved, deliverance will have to come from 'another quarter' (cf. 4:14). The new wrinkle in human wickedness will have to be met with a fresh twist of divine providence. 'On that night the king could not sleep' (6:1) – unseen divine fingers quietly propped open royal eyelids. Naturally, there is theology in such tension: God frequently uses human servants who risk everything as his instruments of deliverance; but sometimes no human means can help and he delights to bring deliverance by his own unaided, secretly working hand. Insomnia and salvation. Sometimes God insists on bringing deliverance all by himself – and yet he makes it look so natural.

Let's take another example: Exodus 2:1-10. Exodus 1, of course, ends on a tense note. Pharaoh has been frustrated one way or another in Exodus 1 in his mission of decimating Israel; so, at last, he authorizes all his people as deputies and decrees that every Hebrew baby boy is to be chucked into the Nile (1:22). So what will happen in the case of this particular Hebrew couple (2:1)? The whole account follows a sort of chiastic pattern:

Mother, vv. 2-3
Sister, v. 4
Daughter of Pharaoh, vv. 5-6
Sister, vv. 7-8
Mother, vv. 9-10

In light of 1:22 the very birth of a son (2:2) sends chills up our spine. Tension intensifies when the baby becomes unhide-able (2:3). So his mother goes to work making an 'ark' (see Gen. 6–9!) for him. Perhaps she had observed the bathing habits of Pharaoh's daughter? Perhaps she assumed pagan religion might be useful, i.e., if an Egyptian girl finds the infant in the Nile, would that girl perhaps infer that the Nile-god was protecting the infant? All of this we don't know. But at the center of our episode (see above), at verses 5-6, the suspense becomes agonizing. If we had musical scores to go along with narratives, we would hear a very pins-and-needles piece here. Actually, the written text elevates our blood pressure all by itself, since the grammar and syntax become a bit choppy:

> (5)And the daughter of Pharaoh went down to bathe at the Nile, and her maids were walking along beside the Nile; then she spotted the ark among the reeds; and she sent her servant girl to get it.
> (6)And she opened (it), and she saw him – the child; and, oh, the lad was crying. And she felt pity for him, and said, 'This is one of the Hebrews' children.'

Opening, seeing, crying, feeling – the text captures every movement in this dread-laden moment. Of course, there is much more in Exodus 2:1-10 than this literary anxiety. But this tension is not some mere literary device; it is a theological primer. It tells us that sometimes Yahweh's providence is a heart-stopping providence. In fact, it tells us something important about God – he is not boring; he is able to keep you interested. He may perplex you; he may even drive you to despair; he may keep you on the edge of your seat far longer than you want – but no one who knows him will ever call the God of the Bible boring.

I started the chapter with my little, red Ford pick-up, and it's only proper we should end with it. Have you ever noticed that when you drive a certain kind of vehicle you tend to notice others of the same ilk? So I notice other red Ford Ranger pick-ups *without* an extended cab. If you've a Toyota Corolla, same thing. That, I think, is the value of 'owning' certain literary 'quirks' of Old Testament narrative. If you become familiar with them, you will notice them when they occur in other texts. Are these all the literary features of narrative? By no means. I haven't even tried to supply that. This is a kind of home-made list concocted out of my own study. But, hopefully, noting these will make us better observers, help us recognize where such features occur in other passages, and simply stir our juices for the study of narrative.

Endnotes

1. Walter C. Kaiser, Jr., 'Narrative,' in *Cracking Old Testament Codes*, ed. D. Brent Sandy and Ronald L. Giese, Jr. (Nashville: Broadman & Holman, 1995), 70. Block sums up the whole dilemma well with an excellent programme for solving it: 'But biblical *narratives* pose special challenges for those who seek the authoritative meaning. Whereas in didactic (e.g., "You shall love the LORD your God with all your heart") and many forms of lyrical texts ("The heavens are telling the glory of God") the intended message is declared explicitly, in narrative the permanent lesson is often, if not generally, implicit in the telling. With respect to short stories like the Book of Ruth, which are at the same time historiographic in nature, the biblical narrator's aim is never merely to recreate or reconstruct past events. And we have not fulfilled the demands of the text even when we, in our minds, have come to recognize exactly what has happened. In the Scriptures historiographic compositions are primarily ideological in purpose. The authoritative meaning of the author is not found in the event described but in the author's interpretation of the event, that is, his understanding of their [sic] causes, nature, and consequences. But that interpretation must be deduced from the telling. How is this achieved? By asking the right questions of the text: (1) What does this account tell us about God? (2) What does it tell us about the human condition? (3) What does it tell us of the world? (4) What does it tell us of the people of God – their collective relationship with him? (5) What does it tell us of the individual believer's life of faith? These questions may be answered by careful attention to the words employed and the syntax exploited to tell the story. But they also require a

cautious and disciplined reading between the lines, for what is left unstated also reflects an ideological perspective' (Daniel I. Block, *Judges, Ruth*, New American Commentary [Nashville: Broadman & Holman, 1999], 604-605).

2. It should also help us to view Job correctly and sympathetically throughout the book. As we read/listen to his speeches we must think: here is a man who has been devastated and who does not know what I, the reader, know about his case. The three friends and Elihu did not have 1:6-12 and 2:1-7a – and look what a mess they made of Job's trouble.

3. In *Secrets and Spies: Behind-the-Scenes Stories of World War II* (Pleasantville, NY: Reader's Digest, 1964), 136-37.

4. Sometimes a writer omits for economy's sake. Observe the information gap between 2 Kings 1:4 and 1:5. The writer doesn't fill in all the informational details between the two verses; he assumes intelligent readers will supply them mentally.

5. One could say the writer of Hebrews uses this sort of technique in Hebrews 11:32-40. He doesn't simply say, 'Living by faith can be both marvelous and nasty,' but barrages us with concrete instances that help us see his point in living color.

6. Fleeing from 'the presence of Yahweh' doesn't mean Jonah never exegeted Psalm 139 in seminary. Jonah wasn't stupid. He knew of Yahweh's universal sway (see 1:9!). But I understand his action in light of the language of 1 Kings 17:1 and 2 Kings 5:16, where Elijah and Elisha refer to Yahweh as the One 'before whom I stand,' i.e., a prophet who 'stands' in Yahweh's presence, receives his orders, and is ready to carry out Yahweh's directions. It is that calling and that service Jonah wants to forego. Jonah wants no part of Project Nineveh, and, if he is no longer in the land, perhaps Yahweh will find someone else. He doesn't think he can get beyond God's sovereign sway – he simply wants to get away from God's immediate call. 'Fleeing' from Yahweh's presence means fleeing from his office as prophet. Many assume (gratuitously?) that Jonah stands for Israel and for her narrow attitude toward the nations' inclusion in God's mercy. But who can prove that Jonah is an allegorical cipher for Israel? Maybe the Book of Jonah is about Jonah! About a prophet's call and ministry. Cf. C. Hassell Bullock, *An Introduction to the Old Testament Prophetic Books* (Chicago: Moody, 1986), 42, 53-54; and Alec Motyer, *The Story of the Old Testament* (Grand Rapids: Baker, 2001), 111.

7. Lewis Drummond, *Spurgeon: Prince of Preachers* (Grand Rapids: Kregel, 1992), 204-205.

8. See my *Joshua: No Falling Words* (Ross-shire: Christian Focus, 2000), 188-97.

CHAPTER 3

Theology

Despair may have begun creeping over you as you saw the word – 'theology.' Here's the thick, heavy stuff, you say. But I don't know what's wrong with theology. It's what we live for, isn't it? In any case, I'm using the term here to refer to the theology of a biblical text, that is, what the text means to say about God, his ways and his works. Or, to put it a bit differently, I use the term to refer to the *intended message* of a biblical text. I do not want to discuss how one detects the intention of a text here – I touched on that via a few inadequate hints in chapter 1. Rather, I want to focus on a section of material (the 'patriarchal' narratives in Genesis) in which an initial, premier passage (Gen. 12:1-9) determines the meaning of so many of its individual passages.[1] There are reasons for taking this approach: (1) it will allow us to stay within one block of textual material, while mining for the theology of texts; (2) it will illustrate how preceding biblical theology helps to interpret subsequent passages; and (3) I'm writing the book and should be allowed to do what I want.

The Quad Promise

Here we start with Genesis 12. And that is a problem because no sane person can explain why there is a Genesis 12. Well, go back to Genesis 1–11. There you run into the three-fold crisis of the Fall (ch. 3), the Flood (chs. 6–9), and the tower (ch. 11). There you find a world that is repeatedly pleased to do without Yahweh's kingship and fellowship, a world that was then cursed, destroyed, and scattered. After Genesis 1-11, the end should come; the Judge should appear; the lava of divine judgment should petrify the world. Why does Yahweh give to this world that mocks, defies, and rejects him a promise of blessing (the root for 'bless' is used five times in 12:2-3)? God insists on blessing this world with Abraham (and his seed) as the channel of blessing; Yahweh will start yet again with one man as the funnel of redemption until the time when it is clear that the slaughtered Lamb has purchased and preserved a church from every tribe and tongue and people and nation (cf. Rev. 5:9). But it's inexplicable: why should Yahweh give a rip about this world?

But it's even worse. We can't explain Genesis 12 *historically*, shall we say, but neither can we explain it *personally*. That is, why Abraham? Mention the name and folks conjure up kind, grandfatherly images or think of a sort of Jimmy Stewart of the Bible, a genial, kindly, well-disposed sort of chap. But Joshua 24:2-3 knocks that on the head: 'They [the 'they' includes Abraham] served other gods.' So why does Yahweh call Abraham? Why Abraham the sinner, Abraham the pagan, Abraham the idolater? We are beyond the range of reason and awash in grace in this one.

Here then in Genesis 12, and mostly in the first three verses, we have the revelation of what I call the Quad Promise because of its four major components. Let me summarize it in chart form:

The Quad Promise
Genesis 12

People [seed]
> 'I will make you into a great nation' (v. 2)
> 'To your seed...' (v. 7)

Protection / Presence
> 'I will bless your blessers and the one despising you I will curse' (v. 3a)

Programme
> 'In you all the families of the ground will be blessed' (v. 3b)

Place
> 'To the land that I will show you' (v. 1)
> 'To your seed I will give this land' (v. 7)

As you read through the following narratives you will not always find all four elements of the promise mentioned together (although note the 'full' versions in 26:3-5 and 28:13-15) but will meet one or another in line with the concern of the story. I want to touch on some of these subsequent narratives in order to show how the Quad Promise helps us interpret them, or at least keeps us from misinterpreting them.

A beautiful wife is a problem (Genesis 12:10-20)

Abram came into the land and now, apparently, has to leave the land (v. 10). He goes to Egypt. This is a problem – not Egypt but Sarai; she's a real doll and Abram tells her so (v. 11). Yet here is peril: the Egyptian males will be so eager to have Sarai that they will knock off Abram (v. 12). Sarai alive-Abram dead is hardly a recipe for fulfilling God's promises. Hence the policy: Sarai is to pass herself off as Abram's sister and this will save Abram's skin (v. 13). This was an intentional deception but a partial truth (cf. 20:12).

We can get awash in speculation, thinking about the 'probablies' and 'what-ifs.' One might say Abram was exercising a bit of faith here in that he recognized that if the promise of the seed (people) and of the land (place) was to come to pass, he himself had to live! But why throw Sarai to the dogs (or, to the Egyptians)? He is certainly endangering her, putting her in a risky situation. It may be, as some have suggested, that Abram was calculating on buying time. Should anyone want to marry his 'sister,' Abram could bargain along, use delay tactics, and so on. He would have time to finagle. Where Abram's plan may have gone aruck is that he hadn't counted on *Pharaoh* drooling over Sarai and simply *taking* her, as kings have a habit of doing (v. 15). Give Abram credit for a bit of savvy; basically, what Abram predicted in verses 11-13 happened in verses 14-16. He was no dummy. We could say that he was accurate but not faithful; he was almost entirely right and at the same time grossly wrong.

Back to hermeneutics. What is Abram's major defect here? Not lying; please don't moralize the story into a little lesson with which to threaten seven-year-olds. But a failure to *believe* the promise of verse 3a and a failure to rub it into his circumstances. 'I will bless your blessers, and the one despising you I will curse' is the protection-clause of the promise. Protection should be left in Yahweh's hands. The promise of God should have cast out the fear of man. But Abram says, No, no; God's promise is not enough here – this situation calls for my ingenuity. He had Yahweh's promise but did not let it control him in his scary situation (sound familiar?).[2] So 12:3a makes it clear that the problem in 12:10-20 is not with Abram's ethics but with his unbelief.[3]

Now we can't expound this passage completely, but we should not end this little foray without bringing verse 17 and Yahweh's intervention into tandem with Abram's failure. Who knows what the 'great plagues' were that Yahweh inflicted? Maybe obvious infertility? Or illness? How exactly did Pharaoh get the point? Don't know. But Yahweh was true to his word in verse 3a: You mess with Abram, you answer to me. So 12:10-20 should infect God's people with both humility and hope. How, we might ask, can Abram be preserved in a hostile world, so that he will have seed that will multiply and be the channel by which God's blessing comes on the whole earth? Well, not by Abram's smarts. This was a fainting fit of faith. Not so unusual. God has been making new beginnings all through Genesis so far: in chapter 4 after the Fall, in Adam and Seth in chapter 5, in Noah in chapter 9, and now with Abram in chapter 12. But they all go to pot. *And Yahweh's Abraham-plan would have gone down the sewer too except*

that Yahweh determined that by his power he would make
it succeed, in spite of the failures of his servant. That is still
the case. The church must understand that God's plan and
God's kingdom will come because God will see to it and not
because we are such outstanding members of Jesus' varsity
squad. So you read in 12:10-20 of faith's fainting fit, and yet
the account of it increases our hope rather than multiplying
our despair!

A grave hope (Genesis 23)

When we get to Genesis 23 we may give it the once-over and
conclude that it's very sad but of no major moment. It's sad in
that Sarah dies, but most of the chapter is hurry-up wheeling
and dealing with the Hittites for a burial spot (vv. 3-18). Hard
to get excited over reading the record of real estate transactions.
Of course, quick burial was an urgent matter in that climate.
And it's a wonder that today's funeral directors have not
purloined Genesis 23 for their advertising! You can almost
see them fuming, exasperated with Abraham's last minute
arrangements, and then turning to you with their pitch: See why
you need to take advantage of our 'early bird' specials and nail
down your funeral plans under our pre-arranged programme?
You let these things go on and on and, like Abraham, you end
up paying through the nose to the Hittites.

But Near Eastern business transactions are fun to watch
and hear. Abraham makes it clear that he does not want a
'loaner' (cf. v. 6) – he wants his very own burial site. He wants
to make a deal with Ephron for his cave (vv. 8-9). Ephron
insists that a purchase must cover both the field and the cave
(v. 11).[4] Abraham consents, says he'll give the price. 'Price,'
Ephron seems to say, 'did someone mention price? Ah, why
quibble over 400 shekels?' (v. 15). And so it was a deal (v. 16)
and properly attested (vv. 17-18).

But what does this have to do with anything? We back
up. Notice the terminology at the 'book ends' of the chapter,
verses 2 and 19: the specification *in the land of Canaan*. Then

note the repeated reference to 'possession' or property in verses 4, 9, 18, and 20. (Different Hebrew word in verse 18, but same concept). This is a direct-connect with the place-component of the Quad Promise; note especially 12:5-7. Already (here in ch. 23) the promise of the land is *beginning* to be fulfilled! Oh, it's not much. Only a cemetery. But all the same it's part of the real estate Yahweh had promised Abraham. Small beginnings can nevertheless pack big whallops.

Suppose there's an evening meeting of a Christian fellowship on a university campus. Say it dismisses about 9:30 or 10:00. At last there are just several students around talking and, as an act of courtesy, one of the fellows offers to walk one of the girls back to her dormitory across campus. It's a lovely, somewhat crisp October night and they chat as they walk, stop a few moments and watch the ducks near the campus pond. Next day she sends the fellow a thank-you note through campus mail, telling him how grateful she was for his thoughtfulness in accompanying her to her dorm the previous night and including the line 'I had a perfectly marvelous time' relative to the matter. Now what will that fellow make of that? I will tell you. He will be studying late for his European History exam and he will slide that note out of his backpack and read over those six haunting words. Twelve minutes later he resumes study. During a lecture on English literature he opens up that note inside his book and stares at those words while the prof's voice seems to fade. Just a small thing. Only a passing comment. But fuel enough in that to keep him going for two or three weeks until he can stir up his courage to ask the girl out. And what brought it on? Simply a short sentence that he couldn't shake.

That is the way Genesis 23 is meant to operate: to whet our appetite and stir our juices by showing us the tiny beginning of God's fidelity to his promise. And having recognized this, we begin to realize that this is a repeating *pattern* with our God. In the darkest and saddest of times, doesn't he frequently give that small token, that miniscule assurance that certifies that he has not forgotten us?

A beautiful wife is still a problem (Genesis 26)

Genesis 26 nicely breaks down into four sections with a focus word occurring in the first and last verse of each section; hence:

Vv. 1-6	Gerar … Gerar
Vv. 7-11	wife … wife
Vv. 12-22	land … land
Vv. 23-33	Beersheba … Beersheba

We can't work through the whole story, but let's get a taste of it. And what strikes us immediately is that Isaac's problems are the same as Abraham's. There's a famine (v. 1), and the writer clearly distinguishes it from the one in Abraham's time (12:10). It's as if he is saying, 'Don't think I'm some sort of nincompoop who is multiplying famine traditions – this was a different one.' Then there is the problem of his wife: like Sarah, Rebekah is both beautiful (v. 7) and barren. Now the latter is an inference. I am assuming that the events of chapter 26 happened *before* the birth of Jacob and Esau reported in 25:24-26. Biblical narrative is not rigidly or religiously chronological, and it's more likely Isaac could pass Rebekah off as his sister if there weren't a couple of twins running around giving away who Daddy was.[5] Famine and female – Isaac's problems duplicate Abraham's.

But if problems are the same, the text is eager to say that the provisions are the same as well. When Yahweh appears to Isaac (vv. 2-3a), he tells him not to take the Egyptian option but to stay in Gerar-land. And then he assures Isaac by running over every provision of our 'Quad Promise': (1) presence, 3a; (2) place, 3b, 4b; (3) people, 4a; and (4) programme, 4c. The first note is perhaps the most striking: 'Sojourn in this land and I will be with you' (v. 3a). It's the assurance of the Immanuel God that settles his beleaguered servants throughout redemptive history (cf. Exod. 3:12; Josh. 1:5; Judg. 6:16; Acts 18:9-10). 'Sojourn...and I will be with you.' You may be away from your home base, but Yahweh is the 'fellow Sojourner,' the pilgrim God who walks along with his pilgrims on their sometimes meandering way.[6]

What is encouraging to us is that Yahweh presses all the provisions of his promise upon Isaac. It's encouraging because Isaac is no Abraham. Isaac, it seems, never gets anything all to himself. In both Genesis 25 and 27 he shares the spotlight with others. Pioneering Abraham, hairy Esau, and slick Jacob all eclipse him. Genesis 26 is the only chapter Isaac gets all to himself – and even here Esau had to get his foot in the last verses (vv. 34-35). But Yahweh gives his full promise even to his ordinary servants.

'Ordinary' Isaac, however, places Rebekah in extraordinary danger (v. 7). He passes off his wife as his sister and thereby places the people-aspect of the promise in jeopardy. The threat may not seem so acute since, unlike Abraham's fiascos (Gen. 12 and 20), it does not come from a ruler but from 'the men of the place.' But who knows whether next Friday night some Gerar merchant will decide he can no longer keep his hands off Rebekah (v. 10)? So Isaac walks in Abraham's rut. But, the text says, if the foolish failure is the same, the faithful protection is the same. That is the witness of verses 7-11.

The protection of 26:7-11 is the same but not boring. Note the difference between Rebekah and Sarah's deliverances. In Abraham and Sarah's case Yahweh intervened directly – plagues on Pharaoh's household (12:17) or in a 'you're-dead-meat-you-know' dream to Abimelech (20:3). Nothing like that with Isaac and Rebekah – it was so, well, natural. One day Abimelech looks out his window and sees Isaac 'making out' with Rebekah (v. 8).[7] The ruse was exposed. One can imagine the following interview: 'Your sister, eh? I've seen a few men kiss their sisters in my day, but they never do it like *that*!' But no divine fireworks. Ablimelech 'just happened' to look out his window one Wednesday after lunch and discover the truth. God is never confined to one method of protection. The protection is the same yet always delightful and surprising.

When Spurgeon was very young and still in his village pastorate at Waterbeach, he had a run-in with an elderly, crabby woman who had a reputation for verbal abuse. As he passed her house one day, she was standing at the gate and began to 'let go' at him. As she opened her barrage, he smiled and replied, 'Yes, thank you; I'm quite well; I hope you are the same.' With this she laid into him again, and Spurgeon, still smiling, said, 'Yes, it does look rather as if it's going to rain; I think I'd better be getting on.' Which led the woman to exclaim, 'Bless the man, he's as deaf as a post; what is the use of storming at him?'[8]

Now I wouldn't have had the creativity to think of that. It was simply brilliant. A wholly different approach. And that is what we catch in watching the covenant God at work – he is so refreshing because he displays such delightful variety in his deliverances. Why should we be surprised to find the Creator so creative?

My main concern, however, with our foray into Genesis 26 is to underscore that, though here we have stepped out of the Abraham section, the concerns of the promise to Abraham are still the concerns of these subsequent texts. Genesis 26 does not intend for you to lament over how children of parents who lie will likely do the same but to hearten you by showing you a God still keeping his promises even when his servants may not be all-stars.

A biblical soap opera (Genesis 29:31-30:24)

A quick sketch of this section may be helpful. Here we have:

> The super-fertility of Leah, 29:31-35
> A blow-up between Jacob and Rachel, 30:1-2
> The Bilhah connection, 30:3-8 (Dan/Naphtali)
> The Zilpah connection, 30:9-13 (Gad/Asher)

Fertility drugs, 30:14-15
Leah rides again, 30:16-21 (Issachar/Zebulun)
Rachel at last, 30:22-24

Well, what do we do with this? Preach on the 'perils of polygamy'? Or conduct a case study of this dysfunctional family with amateur psychological insights? Note that theology wraps the narrative: 29:31 and 30:22. Be sure to pick up the clear theological note in 30:17. These are anchor points; the first points to Yahweh's justice toward those who are despised and the latter two underscore his kindness in listening to our often-twisted prayers.[9] And yet there's more. Isn't the whole focus of the narrative on the births of Jacob's sons? Doesn't this pick up the seed- or people-aspect of Yahweh's promise? So isn't the emphasis on Yahweh's faithfulness, since we've now moved from Abraham to Isaac to Jacob to *eleven sons*? Let's flesh this out a bit.

Pregnancy seems to be such an easy thing for Leah (29:31-35), which drives Rachel nuts with envy. Rachel explodes at Jacob in exasperation and despair (30:1). Jacob, no fountain of sympathy and understanding, throws her frustration back in her own lap. What can he do? The fact that Leah has had four sons by him clearly shows that *he* is not the dud factor in the fertility equation (30:2). All this leads to a baby race as Rachel, soon to be aped by Leah, becomes a disciple of Sarah and tries her own version of the Hagar method (16:1-4), only it's with Bilhah (30:3-8). Leah does the same with her Zilpah (30:9-13) and has Lucky and Happy (Gad and Asher). It all gets quite earthy. Mandrakes were thought to be a kind of fertility drug and Rachel has the gall to ask Leah for some Reuben had secured for his mother. Neglected Leah assents to Rachel's bargain – Rachel gets mandrakes and Leah gets Jacob as 'stud for the night' (30:14-16). Leah goes on 'producing' (30:17-21) until at last Rachel knows what that's like as well (30:22-24).

It seems like sheer bedlam. Conjugal arguments, man-drake madness, bedroom deals, the covenant family in all its dysfunctional splendor. Yet in spite of all the crabbing, strife, conflict, tensions, bickerings, hatreds, and miseries, God is faithful to his promise: here, after all, are eleven sons. Does this mean God approves of having four wives? Does he then justify the envy that keeps pushing for the most fertile female award? No, God's fidelity doesn't sanitize all the cir-cumstances or twistedness of his people. But…in all the slop the seed *is* multiplying. It's not the dust of the earth yet, but it's a lot closer than Abraham and Isaac ever got to it. It's like Samson's hair – in all the noise and confusion you can fail to notice it's been growing (cf. Judg. 16:22).

Who would've ever guessed that a bizarre soap opera would proclaim the faithfulness of God? But that is clearly the case when you see Genesis 29–30 backed up against the people-promise of Genesis 12; that is, as you are meant to see it. And instead of moaning about family breakdown you will proclaim the faithfulness of God from this text. *The chemistry of divine providence takes the sludge and crud and confusion of our doings and makes it the soil that produces the fruit of his faithfulness.* Don't ever be shocked at the human slop God will throw into his compost to serve his faithfulness. Aren't there some of us who look back on a slice of life full of our own rage and stupidity and lusts and yet see now that God was there in all that gunk in quiet faithfulness? Which brings us to the place where all proper hermeneutics should leave us: the adoration of God.

I have tried to show how the various Genesis narratives are controlled by the 'Quad Promise,' and I have tried to do so using less prominent or less 'popular' passages. Most Bible readers, however, will readily observe that the concerns of the 'Quad Promise' walk right on out of the Book of Genesis and pervade subsequent narrative and the Old Testament materials generally. Not only does the 'blessing to the nations' programme crop up in Genesis (one example: Joseph preserving the Egyptians, 47:13-26) but meets us as Jethro (Exod. 18), Rahab (Josh. 2), Ruth (Ruth 1), and Naaman (2 Kings 5) are drawn to the covenant God; even the Philistines, dense as they are, were given a clear revelation of Yahweh's reality (1 Sam. 4-6). No one needs to argue that the people-component continues to dominate Old Testament narrative (e.g., those of Exodus and Numbers, to go no further) or that the place/land-element pervades Joshua, Judges, and 1 Kings 11 through the end of 2 Kings. The presence/protection axis crops up in its own quiet way in Exodus 2:1-10, is the whole point of the tabernacle in Exodus 25–40 (see 25:8), and proves the bastion of Joshua from the first days in the land (Josh. 1 and 5:13-15), to go no further. The Quad Promise is worth carrying around in your hermeneutical hip pocket. Old Testament theologians still quibble over whether there is one 'center' or controlling rubric for summarizing Old Testament teaching. Walter Kaiser interestingly has held that 'promise' is really the organizing principle at the heart of the Old Testament.[10] And many scholars say one can't do that, that it won't work. But I'm not so sure. If it's sin, it's sin in the right direction.

Endnotes

1. Walter C. Kaiser, Jr. (*Toward an Old Testament Theology* [Grand Rapids: Zondervan, 1978], 16, 18-19) refers to the principle or analogy of 'antecedent Scripture,' that is, an earlier passage 'informs' a subsequent one.

2. It's perhaps analogous to Bertrand Russell being pacifist in his principles but pugnacious in his attitude; the principle never trickled down into his demeanor. See Paul Johnson, *Intellectuals* (New York: Harper Perennial, 1988), 204.

3. Throw stones slowly. Don't we have sort of an Abraham-assurance from Jesus in Matthew 10:28-31, and yet don't we know how torturous it is to rub that assurance into our souls in the middle of our people-fearing circumstances?

4. Perhaps this relieved Ephron of 'tax liability'; cf. Victor P. Hamilton, *The Book of Genesis: Chapters 18–50*, New International Commentary on the Old Testament (Grand Rapids: Eerdmans, 1995), 130.

5. See Nahum M. Sarna, *Genesis*, The JPS Torah Commentary (Philadelphia: Jewish Publication Society, 1989), 184.

6. See this in 2 Samuel 7:6-7; cf. my *2 Samuel: Out of Every Adversity* (Ross-shire: Christian Focus, 1999), 71-72.

7. Actually 26:8 contains a word-play on Isaac's own name. If one could resort to a nickname, one could anglicize it as: 'Sport was sporting with Rebekah.'

8. Lewis Drummond, *Spurgeon: Prince of Preachers* (Grand Rapids: Kregel, 1992), 166.

9. One meets more theological notes, but these come from the characters (29:32, 33; 30:6, 18) and so could be right or wrong.

10. See his *Toward an Old Testament Theology* (Grand Rapids: Zondervan, 1978).

CHAPTER 4

Packaging

Ever help someone move? Folks may rent a truck/lorry and ask you and other friends to show at a specific time on a certain day. Who knows what you'll find when you arrive? Perhaps a few boxes packed, an absence of furniture pads, a hodge-podge of clutter thrown in corners, kitchen cabinets not yet emptied, coat hangers strewn on a table. One despairs. Occasionally, however, one bumps into a different scenario: boxes stacked, taped shut, and labeled; pictures and mirrors already wrapped in proper padding and taped; washer, dryer, and refrigerator already disconnected and ready for removal. The latter picture shows someone who planned and took time and care to make moving as painless and frantic-free as possible. Organization and packaging reveal care and thoughtfulness about the whole ordeal. The same is true when one finds biblical narratives that have been carefully 'packaged.' Perhaps the story follows an obvious structure; or perhaps an episode stands next to another episode and suggests a deliberate contrast. Often this 'packaging' of biblical narratives points to a clear design which in turn may turn up sermonic fodder. Biblical stories seldom have that coat-hanger-and-clutter look that some of our friends throw at us on moving day.

I want to discuss this narrative 'packaging' under two headings: placement, which usually involves the position of a passage in relation to another passage, and lay-out, which

tends to focus on the literary structure of a block of text by
itself.

Placement

In his autobiography Helmut Thielicke remembers how he
was smitten by his 'first love' when he was fifteen. Her brother
was a close friend of young Thielicke's and Helmut wanted
him to arrange a kind of 'introduction.' At first the brother
demurred, but then one day indicated that if Thielicke paid
him so much for a ticket to a church lecture, Thielicke could
attend the lecture and see and likely encounter his sister
there. Spruced-up to the hilt and drawn by the magnetic
pull of early love, Thielicke entered the church hall, handing
his ticket to two astonished young ladies at the door. There
were indications that those around were regarding Helmut's
presence with some surprise, but he sloughed these off as due
to his own nervousness on at last getting to meet and speak
with *her* in this venue. He seated himself in the middle of
the crowd in that church hall in Barmen, Germany. There
was a song – and Helmut became aware that his was the
only male voice amid sopranos. In fact, he noted that only
young girls were all around him! It was worse than that. The
local female doctor on the platform then came forward and
delivered a talk on sex education for girls! His friend had
tricked him and, unfortunately, the ground did not open
up and swallow him.[1] But young Helmut Thielicke could
tell you that position (where you are) really does make a
difference.

Brief Relief

I simply want to illustrate this last point with some narrative
texts. Take, for example, 1 Samuel 23:14-18. You may have
often delighted in verse 16: 'And Jonathan, Saul's son, rose up
and went to David at Horesh and strengthened his hand in
God.' A beautiful touch. But if you follow the pattern of the
story, you note that that section, verses 14-18, is set between

two sections in which David & Co. are under dire threat. David had done Saul's work and had delivered the residents of Keilah from Philistine pillaging (vv. 1-5). But Saul had heard David was at Keilah, and the king planned to bag him there (vv. 7-8). The big question was: since David had rescued the people of Keilah from the Philistines, would they, out of gratitude, protect David from Saul's clutches? Or would they, when push came to shove, hand David over to Saul's tender mercies? The answer to the first question was 'No,' that to the second, 'Yes' (vv. 9-13).

Then one notices that right after the 'Jonathan episode' one hears of the betrayal of the men of Ziph (vv. 19-24). They are from David's own tribe but apparently want to ingratiate themselves with Saul (Did they want government jobs?) and so inform Saul that they know precisely where David's brood is and could certainly lead Saul right to him. So, the overall pattern of the story goes like this:

> The slipperiness of Keilah, vv. 7-13
> > The encouragement through Jonathan, vv. 14-18
> The treachery of Ziph, vv. 19-24

Now I know we cannot give a certain answer. But note how Jonathan's act of devotion comes *in between* two sections in which David will experience either ingratitude or betrayal. Now I ask myself as I look at that – what if that Jonathan-sandwich hadn't been there? What if David had simply gone from one (potential) betrayal to another? Would it have been too much? Could he, as it were, have endured going from Keilah to Ziph with no break? One disappointment on top of another? Is this not at least the providence of God? Is it not God's gracious timing to provide someone to hearten his battered servant lest he have sorrow on top of sorrow? Isn't God gracious to interject into the middle of multiple disappointments these moments of encouragement to keep us from utter despair?[2]

Small Potatoes

Take a second example: Genesis 25:12-26. This text consists of two sections set side-by-side, a dull list (vv. 12-18) and a birth story (vv. 19-26). Let's start with the birth story.

What do we have here? Isaac. Isaac and Rebekah. Looks like it's going to be Abraham-and-Sarah, Act II. You can do the math: no children for the first twenty years of their marriage (vv. 20, 26). And then only two. This lights up that 'dull' list in verses 12-18, the non-chosen line of Ishmael. Ishmael had none of Isaac's problem. Ishmael had a full set of twelve sons (vv. 13-16). No problems with fertility or reproduction in Ishmael's clan. But – again – it looks like the covenant line is pretty helpless and hopeless, like it will never get off the ground because of another beautiful but barren woman. Compared to Ishmael, the church can't even succeed in mere biology.

So when one sees Genesis 25:12-18 over against 25:19-26, the picture comes into focus: here is the power and prominence and fertility of the people of this age versus the weakness and helplessness of the covenant line. All of which suggests to us that Christ's people look pretty fragile and flimsy and few amid the success stories of this age. The kingdom is often present only in its mustard-seed form. So don't be overly upset when the church doesn't seem to be 'flourishing,' when she is beaten down and nearly brought to eclipse, when she looks like nothing among the real powers of the world, for God often does things the hard way, the weak way. So we don't look very impressive up against the world? So what else is new? And…so what?

Grace and Disgrace

Second Kings 5 is a delightful story of Yahweh's total sovereignty (vv. 1-2, in 'big' and in 'small' affairs) and of his infuriating grace (vv. 9-12). But Naaman, the strutting Syrian, lost his rage along with his leprosy when he took a bath in the Jordan and found that 'Wash and be clean' was a sure promise not religious propaganda (vv. 13-14). The fingerprints of transforming grace are all over Naaman – in his attitude (note his 'your servant' five times in vv. 15-18), his confession (v. 15b), his resolution (v. 17), and his sensitivity (v. 18). Naaman left both his leprosy and his paganism at the Jordan.

But then you meet this closing clip about Gehazi (vv. 20-27). The writer seems to cast him as a deliberate contrast to Naaman. R. S. Wallace captured it nicely by referring to 'Naaman the Israelite and Gehazi the Syrian,'[3] for that seems to be the case. Here is Elisha's servant breaking the third (v. 20), ninth (v. 22), and tenth commandments (vv. 20, 26). He is not captured by grace but driven by greed – the talent of silver he asks for (v. 22) is equivalent to three hundred years of wages.[4] And Naaman gave him two talents. Some retirement package! However, Gehazi's premier offense was obscuring the grace of God; for Elisha had insisted that Naaman could pay nothing for Yahweh's benefit (v. 16); Elisha wanted Naaman to understand that, unlike the run-of-the-mill deities of the Ancient Near East, Yahweh is not forever looking for a pay-off – one doesn't have to (indeed, cannot) bribe or manipulate him for his benefits. He gives freely, even to Syrians. And Gehazi destroyed it all; he distorted the truth about Yahweh; he obscured Yahweh's grace; he left Naaman to understand that Yahweh was a 'taker' like any old pagan deity; so he receives Naaman's leprosy (v. 27).

The literary placement is so strategic and suggestive: Naaman, the converted pagan, stands side-by-side with Gehazi, the perverted Israelite. In Naaman one sees the triumph of grace and in Gehazi the trashing of grace. The writer makes the double point that grace is both transforming (vv. 15-19) and terrifying (vv. 20-27) and preaches that grace should both thrill us and scare us. And if it does both, we will probably be all right.

Seen and Unseen

Finally, observe how we find Ruth 4:18-22 placed right after 4:14-17, so that we have a kind of 'double ending' at the close of that book. Now 4:18-22 affects how we look at the whole Book of Ruth, but here I simply want to look at it in its position after 4:14-17.

There's a bit of resolution for Naomi in 4:14-17 in the wake of all her previous troubles. Some may get impatient here. Some may say that we need to get our eyes off Naomi, that it's not really about her, that there are 'redemptive-historical' issues in the text and we need to be paying attention to the 'redeemer' (*goʾēl*) motif that points us to Christ, and so on. But God never gets so wrapped up in kingdom affairs that he forgets his kingdom people. Indeed, in the Book of Ruth the Holy Spirit seems to insist that we keep Naomi in view, for in reading Ruth one becomes aware of a certain literary pattern: every major episode returns attention to Naomi. That's not so unusual in chapter 1 – Naomi's return has taken up the whole chapter, so we are not surprised when the closing scene focuses on Naomi and her female friends at the city gate. But it's always that way: Ruth's day in the barley field (ch. 2) closes with her report to Naomi and Naomi's revised 'confession' (2:20 compared to 1:20-21); the thrill and suspense of the threshing-floor (ch. 3) end up in a de-briefing session with Naomi (3:16-18); and even the day in court (ch. 4) closes off with what it all meant for Naomi (4:13-17).

It's fascinating what one finds in church pulpits. Folks in the congregation can't see the junk and clutter often left in these sacred repositories. One Sunday a few years ago I was preaching in a country church in Mississippi and noted that there were two aerosol cans of 'Wasp and Hornet' spray inside the pulpit. I knew what they were for – especially in the spring when the weather starts to warm and the invaders come diving and swooping at morning worship. I couldn't help thinking how I would've loved to have had such weapons years earlier – for I remembered preaching in one of our rural Kansas congregations in the late spring when a wasp or two decided to attend worship. People were doing their best to look me in the eye while I was preaching; but it was a futile effort. I could follow their gaze as they traced a wasp's near plunge before rising again to a safe height. They simply couldn't take their eyes off of the wasp; it preoccupied their attention. Fortunately, it foolishly landed on the pulpit where I smashed it under a lightning right hand, flipped it off on to the carpet, and found people able to concentrate again.

That is the situation with Naomi in the Book of Ruth. Every chapter returns to Naomi *and some provision for her* (even in chapter 1, where Ruth was her unseen provision, 1:22), no matter what the main scene of the chapter seems to be. It's as if the Lord is like my Kansas congregation – he simply can't take his eyes off Naomi; he is preoccupied with her welfare. It's the text's way of saying, Naomi is never forgotten; she is always the focus of Yahweh's attentions.

Now we've just been on a tangent in case you didn't know it. All of that because there will always be a nay-sayer who says it's 'not about Naomi.' But in the Book of Ruth it is – the writer always comes back to her, and so we rightly focus on her here in 4:14-17.

Her lady friends exude praise for Yahweh for what Naomi now has – a *go'l*, a redeemer, one who 'will give you renewed life and be your support and stay in your old age' (v. 15, REB).[5] And they especially wax eloquent over what Naomi *has had* all along – 'a daughter-in-law who loves you' and who is 'better to you than seven sons' (v. 15b). So Naomi is not 'empty' (1:21); she now can enjoy a bit of that joy that comes in the morning after the night of weeping (Ps. 30:5). For a great while she may even have despaired of 'morning,' let alone 'joy.' But now Naomi can see this – with, it seems, a little help from her friends.

But there's something else she can't see. We've a hint of it in the last clause of verse 17 – 'he [Obed] was the father of Jesse, the father of David.' So we won't flush this line down the drain of our memory, the writer expands it in verses 18-22 by summarizing the family line all the way from Perez (Gen. 38!) through Boaz and beyond Naomi & Co. to David. And David is the covenant king (2 Sam. 7), the one through whom Yahweh will establish his kingdom on earth. Even if David's line of kings features a bunch of weak and/or wicked scuzzballs (Jer. 21-22), Yahweh will make sure a 'righteous sprout' (Jer. 23:5-6) comes up in David's line, and to this Jesus he will give 'the throne of his father David, and he will reign over the house of Jacob forever; and of his kingdom there will be no end' (Luke 1:32-33). All this kingdom promise stands there in germ-form when the Book of Ruth ends by sweeping through this family tree from Perez to David.

Verses 18-22 are saying that Yahweh is working his kingdom plan. And the fact that 'Boaz fathered Obed' (v. 21b) is a part of it – which implies that all of Naomi's affliction and trouble has been caught up in and 'worked together' (Rom. 8:28) in the unguessable chemistry of Yahweh's sovereign plan for his world. Now that's something Naomi could not see – how Yahweh would redeem her affliction, using it as a vehicle in bringing his everlasting kingdom. She could see Obed; she could see the unexplainable devotion of Ruth. But when the writer adds his 'Perez addendum' to the book, he is showing us what Naomi could not see. All of which should teach us caution and wisdom: we simply don't know enough, ever, to despair intelligently and completely over our seemingly senseless troubles – or even over our apparently insignificant service. It seems to me that the 'double ending' of the Book of Ruth packs practical help for all of the Lord's Naomis.

Lay-out

Now I want to look at 'packaging' that goes beyond the placement of texts and involves the lay-out of a whole narrative or a combination of narratives.[6] Sometimes an extended piece of text has a discernible literary structure which can prove of immense help in preaching that narrative. In my opinion only a simple literary structure can be plundered for preaching. One sometimes meets highly elaborate and detailed literary lay-outs of passages in journal articles – ones that may be fine-tuned to halves, thirds, or quarters of verses. That sort of thing may be helpful in an academic study but it is too complicated and intricate to be of much use in preaching. As a preacher I must normally be able to explain literary matters orally, clearly, and succinctly and then to highlight their significance. I cannot afford to lose time in explaining cumbersome literary mechanisms in a text. People must be able to follow easily what I point out.

Philistines, God's wonderful toadies

Let's go back to 1 Samuel 23 once more. I want now to look at the chapter as a whole. Reading through the chapter and noticing the parallel between the potential treachery of Keilah (vv. 6-13) and the vicious treachery of Ziph (vv. 19-24a), one begins to wonder if there is a pattern and a symmetry to the whole chapter. Further study of the story suggests a pattern like this:

> Unexpected saviors, vv. 1-5
>> Human faithlessness, vv. 6-13
>>> Divine faithfulness, v. 14
>>> Human faithfulness, vv. 15-18
>> Human treachery, vv. 19-24a
> Unexpected saviors, vv. 24b-28

A brief rundown. Note that the Philistines are the enemy in verses 1-5, while the unexpected saviors are David and his men. It was really Saul's job to carry on the anti-Philistine crusade. The disappointing revelation of verses 6-13 is that, when all the wash is in, the fine citizens of Keilah, grateful as they may be for David's deliverance, will nevertheless hand David & Co. over to Saul. Then follows the double report of God's and Jonathan's fidelity (vv. 14/15-18). Then the men of

Ziph decide to play Judas and go fawning to Saul; with their
help he at last has David within spitting distance – when he
gets an emergency call to deal with another Philistine crisis
(v. 27).

In preaching this passage I would probably not go over
the literary structure line-upon-line. But seeing the overall
structure helps me when I preach verses 24b-28, not so much
to understand but to appreciate these verses. I can see a
certain irony in 24b-28 by themselves, for the Philistines are
Israel's arch-enemies and yet here, by their timely (and don't
we often see Yahweh's providence in his timing?) invasion,
these enemies prove to be David's 'savior.' But having noted
that the story begins with the Philistines in their typical
role (vv. 1-5) helps me revel a bit more in the reversal of
that role as the story ends. There at the first the Philistines,
true to form, attack and plunder Keilah, and David and his
men are the unexpected (and somewhat reluctant) saviors.
But verses 24b-28 depict a far nastier enemy than Philistia
– King Saul bent on smashing Yahweh's anointed one. But
again, unexpected saviors come to the rescue: the Philistines,
the enemies of verses 1-5, have become – in God's delightful,
flip-flop providence – the saviors of David and his band of
near-goners. It's another who-would-have-guessed episode
that should lead to worship.

Something of the same ilk occurred on New Years Day
1945. Hermann Goering ordered his Luftwaffe into an all-
out attack on Allied air fields, hoping to do enough damage
to American and British planes that they would be unable to
supply besieged U. S. troops in the Ardennes. But the mission
enjoyed only limited success. Goering lost something like
150 of the planes he launched to German flak because he did
not notify German gunners about the raid![7] Hence German
gunners knocked German planes out of the sky. German
anti-aircraft batteries did not usually play 'savior' to Allied
forces. Nor did Philistines to Israel – except in the history
that works by Yahweh's chemistry. But that is the delight of

Yahweh's ways: we frequently stand amazed, and sometimes aghast, at the folks and forces he casts in the role of saviors.

The literary lay-out of 1 Samuel 23 plays a servant role in the task of exposition. The correlation and/or parallel between the beginning and the ending of the narrative helps to highlight the contrast and irony, which, hopefully, lead to adoration.

The grand God of sorry captives

Sometimes seeing the literary lay-out of a chunk of material gives one 'handles' for knowing how to begin expounding such a section of texts. For example, seeing the literary scheme of a narrative block may highlight the main themes in it – which won't write a sermon for me but may tell me what my sermon should be about. In all the mass of detail I may be able to detect the keynote.

Let's take Daniel 2–7 as a case in point.[8] And let's go on a quick inductive tour of the bare data, noting the thematic emphases:

Chapter 2:	Tell, interpret, make known, reveal
	Vv. 4, 5, 6, 7, 9, 11, 16, 19, 22, 23, 24, 25, 26,
	27, 28, 29, 30, 36, 45, 47
Chapter 3:	Rescue, save or deliver
	Vv. 15, 17 [twice], 28, 29
Chapter 4:	'Rules' (RSV)
	Vv. 17, 25, 26, 32 (English)
	[= vv. 14, 22, 23, 29 in Aramaic]
	+ preface and tailpiece, vv. 3 and 34f.
	+ 'King of heaven,' v. 37
Chapter 5:	Tell, interpret, explain, mean
	Vv. 7, 8, 12, 15, 16, 17, 26
Chapter 6:	Rescue, save
	Vv. 14 [twice], 16, 20, 27 [three times]
Chapter 7:	Dominion, throne(s), kingdom (RSV)
	Vv. 6, 9 [twice], 12, 14 [five times],
	18 [twice], 22, 23, 26, 27 [five times]

We can condense from this a simple pattern that repeats itself:

Chap. 2	←	God who reveals	→	Chap. 5
Chap. 3	←	God who rescues	→	Chap. 6
Chap. 4	←	God who rules	→	Chap. 7

Here is a pagan world that is pitiful – it is in darkness and has no light and cannot make head nor tail of royal dilemmas nor forecast what is to come (2:1-11; 5:6-9, 15-16). These episodes are put-downs of Babylonian religion, of pagan hokey-pokey, exposing its abject failure to discern what is and what is to come; but here is a God (of captive Israelites) who discloses truth in pagan confusion (chs. 2 and 5). It may be a pitiful world, but it is also an oppressive world, all too willing to swallow up and spit out God's faithful servants – but they have a God who rescues, a God who preserves his hated and despised people from extinction (chs. 3 and 6). If this is an oppressive world that is because it is an arrogant world, where monarchs *de jour* swagger along questing for godhood – but they run slam into a God who overthrows tyranny, the only One who rules (chs. 4 and 7). As I said, seeing this literary development does not put together my sermon, but if it shows me what my sermon on, say Daniel 2, should be about – well then, that's a start! I may have to nail down the details but at least I know the direction.[9]

Nota Bene

One might pass on a copy of an article or letter to a friend and at some point in the margin write 'n.b.' (*nota bene*) – note well. Pay special attention. But one doesn't always have to scribble an 'n.b.' on a page; sometimes someone will draw special attention to a message by its location. My wife is an avid sports enthusiast. There may be a particular college football game on television one evening. I may not have the endurance to stay up until the game concludes and so will go to bed. But very early next morning (while Barbara still sleeps off her football game) I may go in to my desk and see a note on a scratch of paper, giving the final score of the previous night's game, along with, perhaps, some unusual or significant detail that determined the final score. She places this note in the middle of my desk on top of whatever clutter or work I had left there. That way she knows I won't miss it. Now biblical writers can do that with the lay-out of their stories – by putting a piece in a certain place they make their emphasis clear. Sometimes by the structure of their stories they say, 'Now don't miss this.' And, of course, that should help us in preaching.

Let me give just one example, one involving a rather extensive chunk of text – 1 Samuel 27–31.[10] One could capture the overall structure of these five chapters by means of the writer's parallels and/or contrasts:

> David's dilemma: with the enemies of God (27:1-28:2)
> Saul's dilemma: without the word of God (28:3-25)
>
> David's deliverance: saved by the Philistines (chs. 29–30)
> Saul's downfall: destroyed by the Philistines (ch. 31)

Chapter 27 plus 28:1-2 tell the true tale of David's deception and brutality and it all ends with David simmering in the soup he helped create (28:1-2). First Samuel 27 is not the bright spot on David's resumé, though we do understand that he is a desperate man driven to the end of his tether. So he is a Philistine vassal and his deceit of Achish has worked so well that this king has called David and his men up in his latest draft, as the Philistines prepare for an all-out assault on Israel. What to do? How will Israel *ever* accept David as king if he actually marches with the Philistines against his people? How can he dodge the draft and blow his cover with Achish? Ah, David is in one royal mess.

Now the interesting thing is that the writer cuts off David's story at this point. He has told how David has gotten himself into this perfect pickle – and then he leaves him there. At 28:3 he begins to tell about Saul's dilemma. He doesn't pick up David's story until chapter 29, which functions as a huge antacid – the Philistine military brass wouldn't allow Achish to let David and his men go to war, and it was, thankfully, back to Ziklag for David & Co. But the writer refuses to tell you that yet. He allows you to go stewing over David while he tells you about Saul's trouble. In doing so he tramples chronology in the dust. We know this from the map. Saul's trouble in chapter 28 takes place at Shunem and Gilboa (28:4) *the night before* the big battle. The location is a bit southwest of the Sea of Galilee at the east end of the Plain of Esdraelon. David's release from Philistine military service in chapter 29 occurs at the Philistine marshalling yard and staging area of Aphek, which is on the Sharon Plain *on the* (Philistines') *way* to Shunem (29:1a). All this tells us that chapter 29 occurred *before* 28:3-25 but that the writer takes what occurs later (28:3-25) and inserts it 'earlier' in his narrative. Why does he do that?

I think 28:3-25 gives the answer. Saul stares Philistine muscle in the face and, according to custom, asks directions from Yahweh. 'And Yahweh did not answer him' (v. 6). Not by dreams or Urim or prophets. So he has recourse to a medium to gain an audience with the departed Samuel. Why disturb Samuel?, the latter wants to know. 'I am in severe distress; and the Philistines are fighting against me, but *God* [emphatic] has turned away from me and does not answer me...' (v. 15). Here is a man facing the last crisis of his life and he knows God has turned away from him, that he is utterly alone. He has fallen into the hopeless abyss of the silence of God. The one who has defied the Lord's word (cf. 15:22-23) now suffers the withdrawal of that word. There is scarcely a sadder story in Scripture. It really was 'night' (v. 25b) – the darkest of nights. And this, I surmise, is the reason the writer rips 28:3-25 out of chronological sequence and places it right next to David's dilemma in 27:1–28:2 – he wants you to see David's dilemma and Saul's dilemma side-by-side. He wants you to compare them, to ponder them. He wants you to conclude that though David has gotten himself into one major mess it in no way compares with Saul's. Here is a man abandoned to his own resources, with no light from God, whose last testimony is: '*God* has turned away from me.' It's the writer's way of writing 'n.b.' beside Saul's story. It's his way of screaming Hebrews 3:12-13 into your ears. And he makes that point by the way he arranges his text.

Endnotes

1. Helmut Thielicke, *Notes from a Wayfarer* (New York: Paragon, 1995), 42-46.

2. For more detail see my *1 Samuel: Looking on the Heart* (Ross-shire: Christian Focus, 2000), 192-95 (or in the 2005 reprint, pp. 238-41).

3. In his *Elijah and Elisha* (Grand Rapids: Eerdmans, 1957), 135.

4. John H. Walton, Victor H. Matthews, and Mark W. Chavalas, *The IVP Bible Background Commentary: Old Testament* (Downers Grove: InterVarsity, 2000), 391.

5. I agree with Daniel Block – *go'el* here is not used in a technical, legal sense but simply in the practical way the women flesh out in verse 15; see Block, *Judges, Ruth*, New American Commentary (Nashville: Broadman & Holman, 1999), 727.

6. See David A. Dorsey, *The Literary Structure of the Old Testament* (Grand Rapids: Baker, 1999), for numerous examples throughout Old Testament literature.

7. Glenn B. Infield, *Hitler's Secret Life* (New York: Stein and Day, 1979), 247.

8. I realize Daniel 7 is not classed as 'narrative,' but I believe Daniel 2–7 is meant to be taken as a connected complex. I know that goes against the apparent division between historical narrative (chs. 1–6) and apocalyptic visions (chs. 7–12). Moreover, the careful dating of the visions in 7:1, 8:1, 9:1, and 10:1 may argue for taking chapter 7 with chapters 8–12 (cf. 1:1 and 2:1). However, the linguistic pattern of the Book of Daniel (1:1-2:4a in Hebrew; 2:4b–7:28 in Aramaic; 8:1–12:13 in Hebrew) suggests that chapters 2–7 should be kept together. There are some very stimulating studies in the structure of Daniel; see David W. Gooding, 'The Literary Structure of the Book of Daniel and Its Implications,' *Tyndale Bulletin* 32 (1981): 43-79; Joyce Baldwin, *Daniel*, Tyndale Old Testament Commentaries (Leicester: Inter-Varsity, 1978), 59-63 (summarizing Lenglet's work); and Alec Motyer, *The Story of the Old Testament* (Grand Rapids: Baker, 2001), 147-52.

9. I have developed Daniel 2–7 according to its thematic pattern, but one could also look at these chapters via a *pairing pattern* (each two chapters going together), which might look something like this:

Chap. 2   The rule of Babylon is temporary
                (therefore, rejoice in the enduring kingdom)

Chap. 3   But the rule of Babylon may be tyrannical
           (therefore, be prepared to pay the price)

Chap. 4   Proud king who was humbled and feared
Chap. 5   Proud king too stupid to learn

Chap. 6   Fidelity suffers in Persia as well as in Babylon
Chap. 7   Fidelity will suffer in the end

I thought I had seen this development somewhere but have not been able to trace it. I may be to blame for it; if I have plagiarized, it is an ignorant rather than a vicious plagiarism.

10. For more detail, cf. my *1 Samuel: Looking on the Heart* (Ross-shire: Christian Focus, 2000), 236-39(or in the 2005 reprint 293-96).

CHAPTER 5

Nasties

I may have read it in one of his books. Or I may have heard it in one of his seminars. At any rate I can still hear John Bright's rich, cigar-laden voice declaring, 'There are no non-theological texts in the Bible.' Which means all are fair game for preaching. But you'd never know it. It almost seems like some ogre once promulgated an unwritten decree that certain texts are off limits for preaching. Naturally, most of them are Old Testament texts. Some apparently think that though God allowed these accounts in his written word, he must have higher standards for the preached word. The problem is…well, they are simply nasty narratives.

Now what qualifies a text as a nasty text? Oh, it may be *too dull*. Genealogies and such. But one rebels at this. I've never found them unpreachable. In fact, last year on the Sunday before Christmas I preached on 1 Chronicles 1–9, 'A Whole Bunch of Dead Folks for Christmas.' We were, I am confident, the only church in the whole USA that carried 1 Chronicles 9:1b-4 on its bulletin cover. Even Uthai deserves his day in the sun! Narratives themselves, however, are not usually considered dull. Yet the book of Ezra is narrative (even though it uses lists and letters), and preachers generally are not tempted by it. Perhaps it is dull?

But there are more grievous problems. A narrative may be *too racy*. Why burden oneself trying to explain the twisted morals of Genesis 38? Or it may be *too gory*.

What possibly redeeming social value could accrue from following the writer's zoom lens on Ehud's knife and Eglon's mess (Judg. 3:12-30)? And some are nasty because they are *too severe*. How can we explain fire from heaven reducing servants of the state to puddles of carbon in 2 Kings 1? How can God allow himself to get caught in something like that? Of course, if we stick with a few psalms and a couple of messianic prophecies as our essential Old Testament, we will never have to grapple with this stuff – provided our people don't *read* the Old Testament and ask us about it all.

But avoidance gets us nowhere and impoverishes the church. Naturally we can struggle with how to preach the offense and strangeness of the Bible. However, I have found that 'leprous' texts ('leprous' because offensive or strange) contain hidden treasure. That's why, for example, you can explain atonement from 2 Samuel 21:1-14, or expound a proper approach to worship from 2 Samuel 6, or comfort a battered church from 1 Samuel 15 or Judges 3, or placard the depravity of sin from Judges 19.

We obviously cannot discuss all the 'nasty narratives' of the Old Testament in a brief chapter. But we can treat some samples of what is indiscreet, shocking, bizarre, and baffling and hope our pages will be littered with clues for how to approach such passages.

Indecently Nasty (Genesis 38)

H. C. Leupold wrote a commentary on Genesis about 1942 – not a bad commentary by the way. At the end of each major segment he included a paragraph marked 'Homiletical Suggestions.' At the end of Genesis 38 this section contains only one sentence, which begins: 'Entirely unsuited to homiletical use.'[1] Translated, that means: Don't you dare preach on it! Well, that has the same effect as decreeing prohibition over a rack of warm cookies. It tempts us. And rightly so. Difficult texts should tempt you to preach them. Still, one could almost understand someone looking at

Genesis 38, turning to Paul, and saying, 'Are you *sure* about that bit that "All scripture is...profitable"?'

Where to begin with Genesis 38? First off, we must be clear that this narrative is not literary pornography; that is, because the Bible relates the story does not mean it approves or recommends all that takes place in it. That should be obvious, but apparently it never dawns on some readers. And we needn't worry about critics who charge that this story has 'no relation' with the Joseph story in which it is embedded; there are quite a number of literary and thematic links (some of them contrasts) with both chapters 37 and 39.[2] Sometimes we can begin by trying to take our people along with us in unpuzzling such a narrative; we simply come up to the story and ask, 'Why is this told?', or 'What does it teach?' And some answers begin to pop up.

The trustworthiness of God's word

Judah probably hoped Tamar would simply wither away on the biological shelf; he likely had no intention of giving Shelah to her (v. 11). His tryst with the unknown (to him) harlot was a fiasco of lust (vv. 15-16a) – and stupidity, as he gave her his 'identification cards' (v. 18) and yet did not bother to get her name (vv. 20-22).[3] Anonymous intimacy. He may have assumed he was shacking up with a Canaanite cult prostitute (which may be the import of the word *qedesa* in vv. 21-22) but that was no deterrent. Judah's blind and blatant hypocrisy (v. 24) fits perfectly into Tamar's design, as she plays her trump card (vv. 25-26). Here is a lurid moral mess conducted by one of the fathers in Israel.

What is so astounding is that it is *told*. The lying and lechery, the warts and wickedness, are all there. No one gave the biblical writer hush money. We know history has its share of cover-ups – like the inscription in Holy Trinity Church, St. Andrews, that glows over Archbishop James Sharp as a 'most holy martyr' and 'an example of piety, and angel of peace, an oracle of wisdom, and the personification of dignity.'[4]

How anyone could say that of such an incarnate specimen of ecclesiastical scum is beyond us. That is propaganda. But Genesis 38 will have none of it. Yet Israel had every reason, I suppose, to launder her traditions of the nation's fathers. Why besmirch her past by telling the seamy, unvarnished truth about her ancestors? But the fact that she did tell tells me I can trust this record; this is a book that dares to let the truth fall where it will.

The severity of God's judgment (vv. 6-11)

Some readers may be as distressed over God's severity with Judah's sons as with Judah's fling with Tamar. Yahweh put both Er (v. 7) and Onan to death (v. 10). Er was 'evil in Yahweh's eyes,' and what Onan had done was 'evil in Yahweh's eyes.' Onan essentially refused the role of the brother-in-law in the levirate marriage custom and used coitus interruptus as his contraceptive of choice. In the context of Genesis this 'contravened the spirit of 1:28, the letter of the levirate custom and the promise to the patriarchs, who had been assured they would have numberless descendants.'[5] There's no detail at all about Er, only that he was 'evil in Yahweh's eyes.' That 'Yahweh put (them) to death' seems so preemptory, I suppose, so arbitrary, so abrupt, so non-optional, so intolerant. (And so Yahweh has sinned against the spirit of our age.) But none of this really matters. God does not owe us more information on Er. Some may think Onan's offense trivial but Shorter Catechism people know better: Q. 84 – What doth every sin deserve? Answer: Every sin deserveth God's wrath and curse, both in this life, and that which is to come. Judgment must always be just and, by its nature, will frequently be severe.

If people have difficulty with God's judgment here, it is, I think, a matter of taste rather than substance. They will likely raise the bogey of the 'Old Testament god,' blowing people away for the slightest offense and dropping folks in their tracks for minor slips. But it's all a smokescreen by folks who don't read the whole Bible. What do they do with the

'New Testament god' who arranges a double funeral because folks fudged about a real estate deal (Acts 5:1-11)? Why did folks at Corinth end up in the ER or the morgue because of a little arrogance at the Lord's supper (1 Cor. 11:30)? Why the 'severity' of Hebrews 10:26-31 and 12:18-29? 'Difficulties' with Old Testament narrative often reveal more about us than about the Old Testament. We tend to get irritated if God doesn't fit our notions of what he ought to be. We don't, truth be told, want some God we have to *fear*. Which is to say, we don't want the real God.

The separation of God's people

I think the narrative teaches this point. The yellow caution light begins blinking from the beginning: Judah 'went down from his brothers' (v. 1) – he is putting space between himself and Jacob's clan. He cozies up to Hirah (v. 1), who is apparently a Canaanite. He marries a Canaanite woman (v. 2). He is not adverse to dallying with one who may have passed herself off as a Canaanite 'holy whore' (vv. 16, 18b, 21-22). The writer hardly endorses Judah's conduct. Throughout Genesis he has raised the flag about the necessity of the covenant family's separation: chapter 13, Lot snuggles up to Sodom; 14:17-24, Abram renounces the sovereignty of the king of Sodom; chapter 19, Lot's losses because of his Sodom connection; chapter 24, Abraham's absolute prohibition on Isaac's marrying a Canaanite girl; chapter 34, the peril of Jacob's clan intermarrying with the Shechemites. Clearly he disapproves of Judah's fiasco here, for he shows by contrast the proper response via Joseph in the next chapter (39:7-12).

So here is Jacob's family once more in danger of becoming simply another indistinguishable feature of the landscape of paganism. Hence the writer's rationale for telling this lurid story; he tells a nasty story to show how nasty this people had become. As Waltke says, by his story he raises the question: 'Who will rescue this family?'[6] It's as if the narrator stands back from his story and exclaims incredulously, 'And you're telling me these folks are the covenant people?' Who can deny that it's an apt word for the church? The sexual behavior of professing Christians is the one arena where holiness often fails to leave its mark.

The triumph of God's grace (vv. 27-30)

Judah is quick with the death verdict when he gets wind of Tamar's 'immorality' – and pregnancy (v. 24). But Judah had no clue that Tamar had a wild card to play. Just as they were stoking the fire she so much as said, 'Here's the driver's license and the Master Card of the fellow who did it' (v. 25). Well, actually, she had Judah's signet and staff, all his identification. She had Judah dead to rights.

So the sordid story played itself out, as sordid stories usually do (vv. 27-30). Twins of all things. So Perez and Zerah (who was, technically, the firstborn) were born; one could call them Breach and Bright, or Smash and Sunny. It seems like this story only delays the Joseph story; but interesting things begin to happen even before Genesis closes. Genesis 49 shows that Judah's clan will have the place of ongoing leadership in Jacob's family (vv. 8-12). The Perez connection surfaces again in Ruth 4 and leads us on to David, the covenant king (Ruth 4:12, 18-22); and then Matthew wraps it all up together and brings it down to Jesus the Messiah in that thrilling family tree on the first page of his Gospel (1:1-17; note esp. v. 3). There is Jesus, the son of Perez, son of Judah by Tamar. Glorious news and rotten stuff side-by-side, and God makes the rotten serve the glorious.

After Stuttgart was bombed in World War II, theologian Helmut Thielicke and his family had to re-locate in a nearby village. They got their remaining possessions loaded on to a van of some sort, but, when they were near a railway station, the drawer containing their china toppled from the van. It was all smashed. Nothing could be done except that Thielicke leaped down and began brushing the bits of china off the road with his feet so they wouldn't damage the tires of the other vehicles. Right at that moment, a bomb exploded a few hundred meters up the road, leaving a large crater. If the Thielickes had not had their mishap with the china, they would likely have been at exactly that spot where the bomb exploded.[7] China smashed, life preserved. That is typical of divine chemistry.

In this tale of Judah's lust and Tamar's scheming, Judah's horizons seem no higher than his sheep's wool, Canaanite friend, and sexual opportunity. Yet Judah's complex sin will not destroy God's singular plan. Rather, God uses it to fulfill his plan. Where sin increased, grace super-multiplied (Rom. 5:20b). This does not excuse sin, as if Genesis 38 is proclaiming: 'Let us fornicate so God can save the world.' But it does say that human sin cannot stop divine grace. God takes the deepest depravity and the grossest messes and makes them conduits of his grace (cf. 1 Cor. 6:9-11). So when all is read and said Luther is probably right: Why did God and the Holy Ghost permit these shameful things to be written? Answer: that no one should be proud of his own righteousness and wisdom – and, again, that no one should despair on account of his sins.[8]

Shockingly Nasty

Some 'nasty narratives' are nasty because they depict God in ways readers do not like. We will take up a couple of samples.

Killer in the Night? (Exodus 4:24-26)

Verse 24 will become our primary concern, but we must try to make a bit of sense of the whole scenario first, a challenge for such an interpreter's nightmare. For example, whom is Yahweh trying 'to put to death' (v. 24)? 'Him,' according to the text. But who is 'him'? Moses? The NIV interprets it that way. Or one of Moses' sons, Gershom or Eliezer? Again, Zipporah takes a flint knife and excises her son's foreskin then 'made it touch his feet.' But whose feet? Those of Moses or of the son?

And, are the feet here the kind that gets corns and bunions, or is the term used, as some suggest, as a figure for the genitals? What was the significance of touching somebody's 'feet' with a lad's foreskin? What did Zipporah mean when she said, apparently to Moses, 'You are a bridegroom of blood to me' (v. 25b)? Are we to take that negatively? That is, that Zipporah finally capitulated after ongoing resistance – so she circumcises her son but is upset over it. Or is her statement primarily positive? That is, Zipporah does what Moses should have done, delivers him (Moses?) from death and returns his life to him – hence, he became a bridegroom acquired through blood. Again, whom did Yahweh 'let go' (v. 26a)? Moses or one of his sons?[9]

In spite of all these this-or-thats several matters seem clear: (1) the passage presupposes Genesis 17:9-14, which teaches the necessity of circumcision as a sign of the covenant; (2) Moses, for whatever reason, neglected this in regard to his son; (3) Yahweh's attack brought conformity to this demand; and (4) we must live obediently under God's covenant if we are to lead God's people in living under it. As to the details, I think Moses himself was the object of the attack[10]-the NIV is interpretive but probably right. Zipporah seems to know where the problem lies. Whether she had opposed her son's circumcision and Moses had acquiesced to her reluctance, or whether Moses had simply neglected it and she made good the error, is hard to know.

What shocks some is probably the view of God in this text. It blows some 21st-century minds to think that the Lord attacks Moses and that over a (to them) relatively minor matter! Given our cultural mind-set, even in the church, it is very easy for someone to look at this text and say: 'That is not the way God is; the God of the Bible would not act that way.' They are, at least, misleading when they say that. What they mean is: 'God, as I conceive of him, would never do that.' But that is just the question, isn't it? Do we worship our conceptions of God or God? So this text is good for us.

We do not understand how Yahweh could be so abrupt, so lethal, with Moses. We get used to thinking that there is a dull predictability about God. Sometimes we may even begin to think that because we follow a certain system of doctrine (e.g., Reformed theology) we therefore know what God will and won't do. And there is a danger among both believers and unbelievers of slopping into this way of thinking that so much as says, 'God would never demand or require of us anything we believe unreasonable; God would never do anything I consider to be against good judgment.' That is a recipe for an idol.

The most shocking part of Exodus 4:24-26 is most useful to me. It forces me to ask if God is free to be who he is, or, do I try to make him my prisoner, subject to what I think he should be? A Christian must keep asking himself: Am I worshiping the God of the Bible or only God as I wish to think of him?[11]

Holy Terror (2 Samuel 6)

It's wonderful when religion is fun. And it was fun in Israel that day when David and others set out to play escort to the ark of Yahweh, to bring it from Kiriath-jearim to Jerusalem. All the stops were pulled out – they were celebrating with glory and gusto (v. 5). What happened next we don't have with photographic clarity. But it seems the oxen pulling the cart stumbled or perhaps slipped the yoke – in any case, they jostled the sacred box and the ark apparently seemed doomed to slide off the cart. Perhaps instinctively Uzzah grabbed hold of it. Too late for the EMTs to do anything. They called the mortician. Verse 7 is the closest we get to an explanation: 'The anger of Yahweh burned against Uzzah, and God struck him down there for his error.'

Does God not explain himself? Not really. In a sense, he already had. He had given Israel the 'manual' on moving all the tabernacle furniture, including the ark. You can check Numbers 4:4-6, 15, 17-20. Basically, the instructions were: no touch, no look, no cart. The ark was to be carried not carted, and no Levite on the carrying crew was to touch it. If God gave a manual for moving tabernacle furniture, why did no one trouble to consult the manual? Is Yahweh at fault because he proved faithful to revelation he had already given? Still, protests come to mind: But Uzzah was only trying to help! Why didn't the Lord cut him some slack? Why so abrupt: why no margin for error – or instinct? Answer: I don't know, and I wager you won't find out either. But I suspect the text is not too interested in satisfying your curiosity. You want to find a satisfactory explanation; the text wants you to see a holy God. Many readers will probably not be satisfied with this response, but I think the Uzzah episode says to us: You can either gripe or tremble; you'll do better to tremble.

But 2 Samuel 6 does not mean to send its readers away shaking and terrified. The whole chapter hinges on a transition (v. 12a), which says that the Lord's presence (signified in the ark) is meant to bring the Lord's blessing to the Lord's people. So the whole chapter breaks down like this:

> Holy terror, vv. 1-11
> Transition, v. 12a
> Delirious joy, vv. 12b-23

The consternation of verses 1-11 gives way to the celebration of verses 12b-23. In one text we are getting both barrels of biblical truth: the presence of God is both dreadful and delightful. So this (partially) nasty text carries a warning for both the casual worshiper (vv. 1-11) and the cold worshiper (vv. 12-23; e.g., Michal, vv. 20-23)

I think the 'nastiness' readers find in 2 Samuel 6 is primarily a subjective nastiness. The problem for most arises out of verse 6-7. That problem is that God has acted in a way we wish he had not acted. God has done what readers do not like. Was he unjust? No – not if one allows Numbers 4 to weigh in. Was he severe? Yes. But if it is a righteous severity, have we any right to complain? We may claim we would have been kinder...but then a question should haunt us: Is the Lord deficient in understanding kindness, or am I deficient in understanding holiness?

Brutally Nasty (Judges 4:17-22)

Some narratives are nasty because of the savagery and deception they depict. Well, that is not all. In a God-centered book like the Old Testament, Yahweh is always there. Hence the perplexity: What possible truck can God have with such deadly schemes and intentional violence? The Ehud (Judg. 3:12-30) and Jael (Judg. 4:17-22) episodes spring immediately to mind, and I will take the latter for a sample in this section.

When the day went against the Canaanites, Sisera abandoned his chariot to save his own skin. Arriving at the camp of Heber the Kenite (Heber's Kedesh may have been on the slopes southwest of the Sea of Galilee – Aharoni) and knowing Jael's husband stood in a covenant agreement with his own master, he naturally expected asylum (v. 17). Jael did all she could to assure him that he had reached his refuge (v. 18). Sisera's requests and directions (vv. 19-20) likely gave him the impression that matters, for the present, were under control. Like modern Bedouin women Jael was in charge of pitching tents – she was as at home with hammer and pegs as with pots and pans. She simply drove this peg into different 'soil' (v. 21). And there he was when Barak came running up, heaving and panting (v. 22).

Phillips Elliott, writing in the old *Interpreter's Bible*, was obviously embarrassed by Jael's exploits:

> The event is like the deceit and murder of Eglon by Ehud (ch. 3). These are rough times of which we are reading, when 'human flesh was cheap.' Such evil deeds cannot be justified or defended; they can only be understood, and that dimly, on the basis of a ruthless age and so intense a concern for Israel's life and faith that whatever contributed to that end

was condoned. Yet even the ancient writers did not regard this act as inspired by God, and when in the early Christian Era the author of the Epistle to the Hebrews compiled his great chapter on faith (Heb. 11) and mentioned many of the judges – Gideon, Barak, Samson, Jephthah – these two who displayed such deceit in their violence, Ehud and Jael, were not mentioned in his list.[12]

But let's try to do more than blush and wring our hands and apologize. What are we to make of Jael's work?

Sometimes we are told (when dealing with Old Testament passages that seem to be 'morally challenged') that we should remember where in redemptive history the account occurs and not judge it by a later and/or 'higher' ethical standard. That is, we shouldn't, for example, expect Jael to pause as she totes hammer and peg and ask, 'What would Jesus do?' Well, fair enough. But we must realize that there *were* moral categories and standards in 1200-1100 BC. They were not just emerging from some evolutionary moral slime. We need to take care that we not overplay some primitive-progressive scheme of moral insight.

And (it should not need to be said) we must not resort to allegorizing or spiritualizing in order to evade the hard questions. I have read an exposition of 'she went softly to him' (v. 21) that claims Jael was a true picture of the Christian evangelist – how gently we ought to conduct ourselves as we carry on the work of evangelism! One could just as well see in Sisera's slurping from Jael's yogurt bowl (v. 19) an image of the Lord's Supper – or of desiring the 'pure milk of the word' (cf. 1 Peter 2:2).

We do better to ask if any principle applies to the case at hand. Perhaps. We must always keep one principle in mind with texts sporting moral difficulties: we may need to distinguish between what the Bible *says* and what the Bible *supports*. It's one thing for the Bible to tell you Jacob had four wives (Gen. 29, 30); that doesn't mean it approves of that. The Bible may report something that it obviously does not advocate. Perhaps that is the case here? Could not God *use* someone (Jael) to eliminate an oppressor of his people and yet *not* necessarily *approve* the way she did it? This seems to be Dan Block's view.[13]

It would be much simpler (more accurately, cleaner) if we could rest there. That way we can rejoice in the deliverance without voting for Jael. But I don't think we can do that. Let me quote my Judges' exposition:

> The problem is that the Bible *does* seem to approve of Jael's act. If we castigate Jael's blow we shall have to censor Deborah's song as well, for Deborah commends Jael (5:24-27) and condemns the town of Meroz (5:23) for doing nothing. This estimate does not seem to be merely Deborah's private opinion, for Meroz is cursed by the authority of (no less than) the Angel of Yahweh.[14]

There's no doubt that in her song Deborah relishes Sisera's demise – she itemizes it in lurid and luscious detail (5:25-27). And she approves of Jael for what she has done – 'Most blessed of women be Jael' (5:24a). If Deborah is speaking as a prophetess (4:4), her view and Yahweh's view must be identical. And no need to shed tears over Sisera. He and his cronies raped Israelite girls (5:30); he then was one of Yahweh's enemies (5:31). And now he has a tent peg through his brain. It's called justice.

Block's view is much simpler. He can walk away from the text with no real problems (except, in my view, missing the implications of Deborah's song). If I am right that the text is pro-Jael, then I still have problems. What, for example, about Jael's deception (4:18-19)? It's there. Maybe I can have an answer for it if I get more insight, but for right now it stays there. My purpose in tackling any 'nasty narrative' is not to relieve myself of all difficulties concerning the story; my goal must be to understand how Scripture itself views the story and to take that position, whatever questions I may still have. Whatever I make of it, Sisera's stiff corpse is a blessed assurance – that's how all of Yahweh's enemies will perish (5:31).[15]

Now someone will complain that I have not dealt with nearly all the 'nasty' narratives. No, I haven't; one can only handle so much nastiness at once. Nor have I even dealt with all the categories of nasty narratives, for the 'unjustly nasty' might merit attention. These are stories that are considered repulsive because, in my view, they have not been properly understood. Samples would be 2 Kings 1:9-18 (fire from heaven) and 2 Kings 2:23-25 (bears and boys). Since I have recently dealt with both of these elsewhere, I omit them here.[16] I only add one bit of counsel: Don't be afraid to wade into the nasty narratives of the Old Testament, for it's in the nasty stuff you'll find the God of scary holiness and incredible grace waiting to reveal himself.

Endnotes

1. H. C. Leupold, *Exposition of Genesis*, 2 vols. (Grand Rapids: Baker, 1942), 2:990.

2. See, e.g., Bruce K. Waltke, *Genesis: A Commentary* (Grand Rapids: Zondervan, 2001), 506-509.

3. On this last cf. Nahum Sarna, *Genesis*, The JPS Torah Commentary (Philadelphia: Jewish Publication Society, 1989), 269.

4. J. D. Douglas, *Light in the North* (Grand Rapids: Eerdmans, 1964), 139.

5. G. J. Wenham, 'Genesis,' *New Bible Commentary*, 4th ed. (Leicester: Inter-Varsity, 1994), 85.

6. Waltke, 506.

7. Helmut Thielicke, *Notes from a Wayfarer* (New York: Paragon House, 1995), 183.

8. In J. P. Lange, *Genesis*, Lange's Commentary on the Holy Scriptures, in vol. 1, *Genesis-Leviticus* (1868; reprint ed., Grand Rapids: Zondervan, 1960), 595.

9. Check the commentaries for more detail; e.g., U. Cassuto, *A Commentary on the Book of Exodus* (Jerusalem: Magnes, 1967), 58-61; John D. Currid, *A Study Commentary on Exodus*, 2 vols. (Darlington: Evangelical, 2000), 1:115-17; John L. Mackay, *Exodus* (Ross-shire: Christian Focus, 2001), 97-99; J. A. Motyer, *The Message of Exodus*, The Bible Speaks Today (Downers Grove: InterVarsity, 2005), 92-95; C. Houtman, *Exodus*, Historical Commentary on the Old Testament, 3 vols. (Kampen: Kok, 1993), 1:432-48.

10. I think the attack was likely some form of direct physical assault (note v. 26a, 'he let him go') rather than an illness (as assumed by many commentators). Cf. the 'opponent' who fought with Jacob (Gen. 32:22-32).

11. There is more in Exodus 4:24-26 than this, but I have wanted to deal with the 'shock' of the text and how this makes us face the freedom of God to be who he is and not what we want to make him. Were I to treat all of Exodus 4, I might do so by highlighting what it reveals about Yahweh, viz., he is…

I.   The God who stoops to sustain our faith, vv. 1-9

II.   The God who is greater than our inadequacies, vv. 10-20

III.   The God who protects us from despair, vv. 21-23

        [by clearly revealing the difficulties we will face]

IV.   The God who destroys our false impressions of him, vv. 24-26

12. *The Interpreter's Bible*, 2:716-17. Elliott's comment reflects its 1950s' origin perhaps. But one still meets this mentality, i.e., that was a barbarous time and we are far more morally refined now – a ludicrous assumption if one only has some idea of what Jesus' people (to look no further) suffer at this time across our world, not to mention the domestic violence and cruelty that pervades 'advanced' cultures today. Elliott also makes a massive inference from silence, as if he expects the writer of Hebrews to include a list of approved judges in a clearly *summarizing* statement (Heb. 11:32).

13. D. I. Block, *Judges, Ruth*, New American Commentary (Nashville: Broadman & Holman, 1999), 209-210.

14. *Judges: Such a Great Salvation* (Ross-shire: Christian Focus, 2000), 79.

15. One should note in Judges 4 that both prophecy and providence lead up to the Jael-segment in verses 17-22. Deborah settles the matter of gender and glory in her prophecy in verse 9: 'into the hand of a woman [emphatic phrase] Yahweh will sell Sisera'. Naturally, that would be thought shameful – for someone like Sisera with all his biceps and tattoos to be decimated by a female. And, a non-Israelite one at that. And so now geography and providence link up with gender and glory: in verse 11 we meet a little 'oh-by-the-way' moving notice. Heber the Kenite moved, perhaps from the south (1:16), to the north, where Mrs. Heber will, strangely enough, be on location to strike the decisive blow.

16. See my *2 Kings: The Power and the Fury* (Ross-shire: Christian Focus, 2005), 19-26, 37-40.

CHAPTER 6

Macroscope

When I move into a new community, especially if it's a town or city of some size, I like to keep a city map handy for obvious reasons. But only a certain kind of map. I usually don't want a highly-detailed one taking up multiple pages. I want something like what one finds in a Road Atlas, where the whole city is laid out on a quarter or half of a page. A map like that is useful precisely because it has to omit so much detail. I don't want to know *all* the streets – only the main arteries. I want something I can mostly memorize, so that I can find my way around. I may get lost but I'll come out at one of the primary streets and get my bearings again. Too much detail can ruin perspective; one needs an overall orientation – bits and pieces can be worked into that later.

There is a carry-over here to the way we come to Old Testament narrative books. We can – and rightly – deal with individual passages within those books; nothing wrong with microscopic Bible study. Details matter. But it helps to see that individual passage in the light of the whole book. It helps to view the particular through the lens of the general. So we need 'maps' of whole books.[1] We need to use our *macro*scope as well. It's what I call the 'glob' approach to Bible study, and I'll try to illustrate via some samples.

Exodus: picking up emphases

If we back away from a biblical book far enough that we can see it whole, we are more likely to pick up emphases and connections the writer wants us to see. We may well miss these if we are only sizing up one pericope or story at a time.

As we walk into Egypt it is obvious that Israel needs deliverance, but Yahweh does not explicitly declare that that is his programme until 3:7-8. Here he gives his people sympathy ('I have surely seen the affliction of my people...I know their sufferings') and promises to give them liberty ('I have come down to deliver them') and stability ('to bring them up...to a good and broad land'). This strikes the keynote for the opening section: Here is Yahweh, the God who delivers.

This theme dominates the first part of Exodus. One could call chapters 1–2 the *prelude* to deliverance, chapters 3–11 the *obstacles* to deliverance (the obstacles being a servant's reluctance, chs. 3–4, and a king's resistance, ch. 5–11, the former met by divine equipment and the latter to be overcome by divine judgment), chapters 12–13 the *sacrament* of deliverance (Passover), and 13:17–15:21 the *experience* of deliverance (hymn titles could summarize the respective segments: 'He leadeth me,' 13:17-22; 'To God be the glory,' ch. 14; 'I will sing of my Redeemer,' 15:1-21). We naturally see deliverance par excellence at the sea in chapter 14 (esp. 14:30), in line with Yahweh's assurance at 6:6.

But how far does the 'deliverance' section go? Are we to think of a new section beginning at 15:22? I think not. Notice that the deliverance language piles up at 18:1, 8-12, the Jethro story. I suggest then that the deliverance section should extend through chapter 18. I think Exodus places a great deal of importance on this Jethro episode, and I want to take some space to look at it in light of what precedes it and even what follows it. If we want to continue our theme, we could dub 15:22-chapter 18 the *struggles* of deliverance.

First off, let's get the content of 15:22-chapter 18 in front of us. It falls out like this:

Three 'provision' episodes, 15:22-17:7
    Water, 15:22-27
        Manna and meat, ch. 16
    Water, 17:1-7
One 'opposition' episode, 17:8-16
Jethro's visit, ch. 18

Let's focus on chapter 18 and make some observations about it. First, the writer (I should think Moses most likely) must have a particular purpose in placing chapter 18 here, because the story seems to be out of chronological order. Jethro arrives at 'the mountain of God' (18:5), i.e., Sinai, so his arrival must have happened *after* 19:1-2. Then note 18:16 and 20 – Moses settles the people's disputes and in the process instructs them in 'the statutes of God and his laws' (v. 16). This seems to presuppose that Moses has *already received* the revelation of Yahweh's law in chapters 19–23. It seems that Jethro's visit actually took place at some point after the Sinai revelation but was 'brought forward' and placed here, apparently for some particular purpose. Any clues as to what that purpose might be?

Let's make a second observation. Note how Jethro's praise in 18:1, 8-12 forms such an appropriate parallel to Israel's praise in 15:1-21. Both are responses to Yahweh's deliverance of his people:

      15:1-21   Song of Israel
      18:1, 8-12   Praise of gentiles

Third, notice that the Jethro account not only parallels Israel's praise but stands in *deliberate contrast* to other episodes that precede it. Look at 18:8-12 in light of what immediately precedes:

In 3 'provision' episodes Israel *murmurs*...
- 15:24
- 16:2, 7 [twice], 8 [3 times], 9, 12
- 17:3
Pagan Amalekites attack and destroy, 17:8-16

The covenant people Israel murmurs in unbelief against Yahweh, while the maverick gentile confesses his faith in Yahweh.[2] The Amalekites attack and try to cut down Israel (17:8-16), but not all pagans, not all gentiles are like that. Here is Jethro who comes to share Israel's faith (18:10-12) and also brings positive benefit to Israel through the counsel he gives Moses (18:13-27).

All of this implies that the writer saw strategic importance in the Jethro story. It suggests that the *climax* of the deliverance section consists of a *gentile* confessing his faith in Yahweh as the supreme and saving God. So Yahweh has not only delivered Israel from bondage but delivered a gentile from blindness. We needn't wait for those stories of Rahab and Ruth and Naaman – already in and with Israel's salvation Yahweh is at work bringing light to the nations. Already he is bringing the riff-raff under the truth of God and into the kingdom of God. And there's the bad news: you can enjoy marvelous experiences of God's power and yet be walking in unbelief. That is the import, for example, of the marked contrast between unbelieving Israel and praising Jethro. Jethro's faith stands over against not only the hatred of Amalek but also the cynicism of Israel and therefore serves as an alarm to those who keep enjoying multiple privileges and yet can't stop bellyaching about God. Sackcloth time for Presbyterians, Baptists, Anglicans, Pentecostals, and such ilk.

There is not likely much debate about the next division of Exodus, chapters 19–24, the covenant at Sinai. Here we meet the giving of the covenant law, both the ten commandments (ch. 20) and more detailed stipulations (chs. 21–23). We should make, however, two general observations about this section. First, chapter 19 forms a rather extended introduction to the giving of the law. Why such a build-up? Why doesn't the Lord just get to the point? Why all the thunder and lightning and smoke and fire? Why this lengthy report of the shaking mountain and trembling people? Why this scariness and intimidation? Why does the Lord make Israel shudder so before he speaks? Because God's holiness must impress God's people if they are to revere God's law. The majesty of God nurtures the fear of God, and so Yahweh 'wastes' a whole chapter getting the people prepared to receive his law.

Our second observation can be a question: What is significant about the fact that God's law is not given until chapters 19 and following? Why are there 18 chapters of 'deliverance' before 5 chapters of 'law'? Exodus is simply giving us the good news: always remember that *the grace of God precedes the law of God*. What Yahweh has *done* comes before what Yahweh *demands*; he gives *redemption* before he imposes *requirements;* he first sets you free, then shows you how a free people are to live.

Proper order is crucial. Occasionally my wife may bake a small cake and I will decide to ice at least part of it. We sometimes buy these small canisters of cake frosting in the grocery store. We may use a bit of one, then put the rest in the fridge. But if you bake the cake, let it cool, and then pull the frosting out of the refrigerator and begin icing the cake – well, you can have a crumby mess. The cold frosting does not spread well, yet may stick to parts of the cake and pull up hunks of it as you insist on spreading the stuff. Even a dense male soon learns that order is important: set the can of frosting out of the fridge maybe an hour or so ahead, let it get down to room temperature, and then see how easily and nicely it slithers under your knife as you ice the cake without mishap. That is the basic but critical point made in the sequence of Exodus: there is a proper order; law-keeping is not a device for obtaining grace, it is merely a response to grace already given. Get that settled and the whole Bible will make sense.

Exodus, then, shows us Yahweh as the God who *delivers* in chapters 1–18 (focus: Yahweh's power) and as the God who *demands* in chapters 19–24 (focus: Yahweh's will) – then in its third major chunk, chapters 25–40, it shows us Yahweh as the God who *dwells* (focus: Yahweh's presence).

Why do chapters 25–40 (or, if you prefer, what chapters 25–40 contain) come last? I think by this the writer is saying that the Red Sea (ch. 14) is not the climax of the Book of Exodus, nor is Mt. Sinai (chs. 19–24) – the Tabernacle with its endlessly tedious record of stakes and curtains, of skins and furniture, of dimensions and materials, is the climax of the book. And 25:8 tells you why. We will never understand the tabernacle unless we catch our pants on this text. 'And they shall make for me a sanctuary, and I shall dwell among them.' So Yahweh's tent will be pitched among Israel's tents. Yahweh makes this same point in 29:45-46 – he brought them out of Egypt *that I might dwell among them.* Sinai is not the goal of Yahweh for his people. Indeed, in the cloud and fire over the tabernacle it will be clear, as I think Alec Motyer has said somewhere, that Sinai has become *portable.* Yahweh is not landlocked at Sinai – he is on the move, tenting among his people. And you see all this fleshed out on site in 40:34-38, the last pericope in the book.

But Israel nearly lost this privilege; she was ready to sell her inheritance for a mess of bovine pottage. See how the structure of chapters 25–40 underscores this tragedy:

> A presence offered, 25:1-9
> > Plan given, 25:10-31:18
> > > A presence forfeited, chs. 32–34
> > Plan executed, 35:1-40:33
> A presence authenticated, 40:34-38

Israel's apostasy via calf worship (32:1-6) made them candidates for annihilation (32:9-10). The last verses of chapters 32, chapter 33, and on into chapter 34 trace a long, arduous process of Mosaic intercession and divine restoration.[3] Moses begs and pleads for this fickle bunch to be restored under Yahweh's covenant. There is judgment (32:25-29) and despair (32:30-32); there is an offer of a 'half-way covenant' (33:1-3) and the ongoing pressure of the mediator for more (33:12-17) – and mercy overflowing (ch. 34). If one reads through these three chapters paragraph-by-agonizing-paragraph, one arrives, nearly exhausted, at chapter 35. And yet that chapter nearly makes you ecstatic – for you read of yarn and linen and tanned rams' skins and anointing oil, and hooks, frames, bars, pillars and bases – all the marvelous furnishings for Yahweh's tent. He will – after all! – dwell among this people. Bible trivia never sounded so good or so interesting.

I think you must see that structure of Exodus 25–40 to appreciate what is happening in this 'tabernacle' section. However, let's come back to the keynote of this material – 'they shall make for me a sanctuary, and I shall dwell among them' (25:8). What does that say to Israel? Simply that Yahweh craves to be among his people. *God cannot get close enough to his people!* This is almost more than we can believe.

And yet we have pale analogues in our own experience. The summer after my third year of college I was both preaching at a rural church in central Kansas and working for one of the farmers in that congregation during the week. I studied very early in the morning, then after breakfast worked all day on the farm, then preached and visited on Sundays. There was zero time for extras. Now what complicated matters was that I had a reasonably serious relationship with a girl friend (later wife) who lived some 180 miles west. It's painful not to be able to see someone like that. I had a friend, working at another church, who also had a girl friend in western Kansas, 25 miles further away than mine. We decided absence was torture. Hence one Sunday afternoon (after our respective services) we left in my car and drove to western Kansas. We arrived at Barbara's house and he took my car on to visit his girl. He returned to pick me up about 2:00 a.m.; we drove back; I pulled into the farm about 6:15, ate breakfast, got on the tractor and went out to disc a field. It was one of those insane things college fellows do, but had you asked us we'd have had a logical reply: 'I just had to be *with her*.'

That's how it is with Yahweh: his desire and his craving for his people never flags. You may look at 25:8 and say to Yahweh, 'But it's a wilderness where those ex-slaves are.' And Yahweh replies, 'Ah, but where my people are is where I want to be, with my tent among their tents. They are on their way to the place I have prepared for them, and I am on my way among them, for I am the traveling God; there is no place my people go where I will not also be – I insist on it!' I know… we can go to the Greek text of John 1:14 and link this with New Testament teaching. But isn't the testimony of Exodus a marvelous assurance in itself? Isn't it just the thing some of Yahweh's battered servants need to hear again? Some of them with shattered dreams and crushing loads are making their way through wilderness-like territory, and their God says, 'I will be camping among you, for I can't stand to be parted from my people.'

Joshua: getting an orientation

Scoping out Exodus highlighted certain emphases the book wants to make, especially in its use of the Jethro story and its tabernacle theology. Sometimes, however, sweeping through a whole book only gives a general perspective that helps one view the smaller portions of the book in a proper way. That is, the 'large view' becomes a kind of control that keeps me from abusing or twisting individual passages. Let's glance at Joshua to see this.

The climax of the Book of Joshua comes at 21:43-45. This summary passage draws a thick black line across the page, summing up the whole book to that point:

> (43) So Yahweh gave to Israel all the land which he swore to give to their fathers – and they possessed it and settled in it.
> (44) And Yahweh gave rest to them all around in line with all he had sworn to their fathers; and not a man from all their enemies stood ground in their presence – all their enemies Yahweh gave into their hand.

(45) Not a word fell [lit.] from all the good word which Yahweh had spoken to the house of Israel; all of it came to pass.[4]

In other words, the writer says, 'Let's all stand and sing "Great Is Thy Faithfulness".' And where do we see Yahweh's faithfulness? Why, in the preceding narratives: in the assurance Yahweh gave Joshua after Moses' funeral (ch. 1); in the grace he shows to a gentile harlot in bringing her to share the faith of – and have a place in – Israel (ch. 2); in the exercise of his power as he brings Israel into the land in face of an 'impossible' obstacle (chs. 3–4); in the victory he repeatedly gave over their enemies (chs. 6, 8, 10, 11); in his wrath by which he led Israel to repentance and restoration (ch. 7); in his wisdom which could have averted Israel's folly (ch. 9); in his admonition to stir them to complete obedience (13:1-7; 18:3ff.). The first 21 chapters come to this crescendo (21:43-45) in which the writer rings the changes on Yahweh's fidelity.[5]

What do we find after 21:43-45? We find chapters 22–24. In this second segment there are three *assemblies* of the people of God or some section of them (22:1; 23:2; 24:1) and in each of them the primary concern is Israel's first-commandment fidelity to Yahweh (22:5, 16, 18, 19, 25, 29, 31; 23:6, 8, 11; 24:14-15, 16, 18, 21, 23, 24). Here the writer is telling Israel to sit down and prayerfully sing 'A Charge to Keep I Have.' Graphically Joshua looks like this:

Great is thy faithfulness
Joshua 1–21   ➡ **21:43-45** ⬅   Joshua 22–24

    Assurance
    Grace
    Power
    Wrath
    Wisdom
    Admonition, etc.

Is this not the same pattern we find in Romans, where 12:1 seems to introduce the only logical response we are to make 'in view of the mercies of God' expounded in chapters 1–11? Does not that first mass of the epistle reach a crescendo at the end of chapter 11 as Joshua does at the end of chapter 21? It is the same pattern:

Joshua and Romans
Joshua 1–21 → **21:43-45** ← Joshua 22–24
Romans 1–11 → **11:33-36** ← Romans 12–16

Over 80 per cent of the Book of Joshua is the story – and/or lists! – of Yahweh's grace and faithfulness that is meant to drive you into a corner, to press you to the only legitimate response one can make – to be a slave of ('to serve') Yahweh. One might say Joshua is a two-point sermon:

I. The Record of Yahweh's Faithfulness, chapters 1–21
II. The Responsibility of Yahweh's People, chapters 22–24

Seeing Joshua this way will not write your sermon for you on any given Joshua text. It only gives you a general orientation for approaching Joshua. It tells you that Joshua follows the usual Old Testament pattern: grace then demand. It also tells you there is a *theme* in the narrative record of chapters 1–21. If you preach any of the passages in that section and get so mired in archaeological, geographical, or historical data that you obscure the testimony to Yahweh's fidelity, then you are misusing and abusing that text. You are going against its intent. Now in a book like Joshua one cannot avoid archaeology, geography, etc. And the preacher will have to look at gobs more of it than ever works its way into a sermon. But a sermon on any passage in chapters 1–21 should leave people exclaiming 'Isn't Yahweh grand?' not 'Aren't sermons dull?'

And then this approach to Joshua tells you that this narrative carries a *claim* – it is never some neutral or detached matter. Chapters 22–24 show the urgent and ongoing response that Yahweh requires of his people in answer to his faithfulness. When I preach Joshua's texts I am not trying primarily to inform or enlighten or clarify but to cram God's people into the handcuffs of gratitude, to pressure them to that commitment that says, 'Love so amazing, so divine, demands my soul, my life, my all.'

Ezra-Nehemiah: running into surprises

You may swallow hard to think of Ezra-Nehemiah as narrative. The document contains what appears to be some pretty dry stuff – lists, reports, letters, archives. And yet it is all cast into a narrative framework, so we can justly treat the whole piece as 'narrative' in one sense. I cannot take space to justify my overall breakdown of Ezra-Nehemiah. I must simply summarize my conclusions about its contents and structure and allow readers to check it against the biblical text.

Ezra and Nehemiah were originally one 'book'; that is why I am treating them together in hyphenated form.[6] The document divides into four major sections:[7] Ezra 1–6, from Cyrus' decree to the rebuilding of the temple; Ezra 7–10, the coming of Ezra and reforms under his direction; Nehemiah 1–6, the coming of Nehemiah and re-building of the city walls; and Nehemiah 7–13, the re-structuring of the community's life. Time-wise Ezra-Nehemiah takes up a bit over a hundred years, from Cyrus' decree (ca. 539 BC) to Nehemiah's second return to Jerusalem (ca. 433ff.). There is one dominant focus in each major block of material. Let me set it out in outline form. The 'Roman' headings characterize each of the sections and I will include some sub-headings to suggest the flow within each section. 'New opportunity under gray skies' might capture the overall tone of the book.

> Breakdown of Ezra-Nehemiah
> I. The New Temple, Ezra 1–6
> 1. A future and a hope, ch. 1

2. The founders of the renewed Israel, ch. 2
3. A new beginning...and a new song, ch. 3
4. Do not wonder, brothers, that the world hates you, ch. 4
5. The King's decree and the kings' decrees, chs. 5–6

II. The New Rule, Ezra 7–10
1. Enjoying the hand of God, chs. 7–8
2. Escaping the wrath of God, chs. 9–10

III. The New City, Nehemiah 1–6
1. The good hand of my God, chs. 1–2
2. The careful record of my workers, ch. 3
3. The great opposition to my work, chs. 4–6

IV. The New Society, Nehemiah 7–13
1. The work of reformation, chs. 7–10
2. The work of consolidation, 11:1-13:3
3. *Always* reforming?, 13:4-31

The last segment is something of a climax and one becomes mildly optimistic about life in Jerusalem after the covenant renewal of Nehemiah 10 and the celebrations of chapter 12. It is then that we meet our surprise: 13:4-31 is a bit of a 'downer' after all the careful, dogged, hard-working effort that has been poured into the Judah Restoration Project to date.

Again, only a brief summary of 13:4-31 must suffice. You must note that the abuses Nehemiah corrects here are ones that cropped up while he was back in Persia (v. 6).[8] They are:

Compromise, vv. 4-9 (cuddling up with pagans)
Neglect, vv. 10-14 (ceasing Levitical support)
Commercialism, vv. 15-22 (abusing the Sabbath)
Amalgamation, vv. 23-31 (intermarrying with pagans)

Nehemiah corrected these abuses with typical vigor and gusto! This section is a clip from his memoirs and so he is telling us of the work he had to do upon returning to Jerusalem: (1) purging impurity, vv. 4-9; (2) renewing the tithes, vv. 10-14; (3) enforcing the Sabbath, vv. 15-22; and (4) disciplining the unfaithful, vv. 23-29. But this is mildly disappointing! At the climax of the book, Nehemiah drops a 'downer' on you because he tells you that the abuses he corrects in 13:4-31 are practices that Judah *had already eschewed in the covenant of 10:30-39.* The people of God may become 'reformed'; they may enter into a solemn covenant – and they are not above breaking every particular of that covenant. Williamson seems to be right on target:

> The Book of Nehemiah seems to peter out in what might be considered a somewhat unsatisfactory manner, not so much with a bang as with a whimper. All the abuses referred to in this final chapter have been the subject of earlier treatment, but they rear their heads again here despite the best efforts of the reformers to eradicate them....It is as though the book is pointing to its own failure, reminding us that however important good structures and routines may be..., nothing can substitute for the renewal of the naturally perverse inclinations of the human heart.[9]

A bit of a surprise. We would hope for something better after all the hardship, prayer, and sheer grinding toil Ezra and Nehemiah had poured into this community. This somewhat anti-climactical ending does not discount the work of Ezra and Nehemiah, but it does expose the flakiness of the professing people of God. Does not the end of Ezra-Nehemiah then function as a blinking, yellow caution-light to those who place too much confidence in reform of the church? Not that such reform must not be pressed. But can't there be a creeping arrogance that gets mixed up with it? 'We will separate from such-and-such a body, and we will start a new denomination, and we will see to it that it remains confessionally orthodox, fosters godly piety, and never gets on that slippery slope to compromise.' But, probably, it will. How hard it is for the professing people of God to remain faithful – even when they enter into solemn covenants to do so. Do you see how Ezra-Nehemiah preaches an *implicit messianism*? Does not the failure of Israel in this chunk of Scripture make you look for the Israelite who will not fail? Covenants are solemnly sworn yet too easily broken. Where will we find the Covenant-keeper except in our faithful Savior, Jesus Christ? Ezra-Nehemiah should drum into us a holy distrust of ourselves, give us a clear grasp of how tenuous our devotion is. 'Prone to wander, Lord, I feel it; prone to leave the God I love.' Isn't it healthy to see that? And if we do, is there not hope? Seeing that in itself should justify the 'macroscopic' study of Scripture.

Endnotes

1. For some samples, see Richard L. Pratt, Jr., *He Gave Us Stories* (Brentwood, TN: Wolgemuth & Hyatt, 1990), 279-305; note how Alec Motyer turns a 'map' of Judges into pay dirt for Old Testament theology – *Look to the Rock* (Leicester: Inter-Varsity, 1996), 23-25.

2. We may have a preview of this back in 2:11-22. It was 'Israel' who rejected Moses' deliverance (2:13-14; see Acts 7:23-28, 35), while it was Reuel/Jethro's daughters who experienced it (2:16-21); the one rejected by Israel is welcomed by Reuel/Jethro.

3. For more detail see my study 'Rebellion, Presence, and Covenant: A Study of Exodus 32–34,' *Westminster Theological Journal* 44 (1982): esp. 75-81.

4. Karl Gutbrod (*Das Buch vom Lande Gottes,* Die Botschaft des alten Testaments, 3rd ed. [Stuttgart: Calwer, 1965], 137) notes that verse 43 (the land where Israel lives) aptly summarizes chapters 13–21, while verse 44 (the conflicts with Israel's enemies) summarizes the victories of chapters 1–12, with verse 45 encompassing the whole narrative of Joshua.

5. 'All' occurs six times in the Hebrew text of 21:43-45.

6. B. S. Childs, *Introduction to the Old Testament as Scripture* (Philadelphia: Fortress, 1979), 626.

7. On this I agree with Childs, 632-33; for a somewhat different breakdown, see Andrew E. Hill and John H. Walton, *A Survey of the Old Testament,* 2nd ed. (Grand Rapids: Zondervan, 2000), 272-76.

8. For those concerned: There is a troubling phrase at the beginning of 13:4. It is usually translated in a temporal sense, as, e.g., in NASB: 'Now prior to this.' This would seem to say that the following episode in which the priest Eliashib gave Tobiah motel accommodations in the temple took place before the episodes of 13:1-3 and 12:44-47. These two last-named sections both begin with 'On that day,' referring to the time of the wall dedication in 12:27-43, and so both these sections are meant to be taken with that time of dedication. Nehemiah was clearly present at that time. However, 13:6 implies that the reason Eliashib checked Tobiah into temple quarters was because Nehemiah was gone, reporting to the king. The simplest solution, I believe, is to follow

the suggestion of Howard Crosby in *Lange's Commentary*. He insists that *weliphne mizzeh* in 13:4 should be taken positionally and not temporally, i.e., it should be translated 'in the face of this,' indicating defiance, not 'before this,' indicating sequence.

9. H. G. M. Williamson, 'Ezra and Nehemiah,' *New Bible Commentary*, 4th ed. (Leicester: Inter-Varsity, 1994), 440. Cf., much to the same effect, Gordon McConville: 'The final note in Ezra-Nehemiah is thus one of ambiguity. We may wonder how the people who had so exuberantly celebrated the completion of the defences against the enemy came so readily to accept the enemy's presence within the Temple and the high priest's family. How, indeed, could those who had committed themselves so solemnly to religious purity (chapter 10) so rapidly return to practices which were essentially irreligious? If we sense a certain desperation about Nehemiah's last efforts to put the house of Israel in order, a tiredness about the need yet again to bring back the wandering sheep to the right path, a feeling that there is no reason to think that this reform will be more successful than any other, a sense that after all he himself has done his best (vv. 14, 22b, 31b), then we may be catching the right meaning here' (*Ezra, Nehemiah, and Esther*, Daily Study Bible [Philadelphia: Westminster, 1985], 149).

CHAPTER 7

Appropriation

Alexander Whyte was writing to a discouraged Methodist minister by name of Jenkins:

> Never think of giving up preaching! The angels around the throne envy you your great work. You [he quotes Jenkins] 'scarcely know how or what to preach.' Look into your own sinful heart, and back into your sinful life, and around on the world full of sin and misery, and open your New Testament, and make application of Christ to yourself and your people...[1]

Application or appropriation of Scripture is not so overwhelmingly difficult if one begins at the right place: 'Look into your own sinful heart, and back into your sinful life.' If a preacher has a lively sense of his own depravity he won't have much trouble applying Scripture. Hence, a la Whyte, use your sinful nature to good advantage – you will apply the word of God in its narrative form much more potently...and graciously.

Now I suppose, I even know, that some say our work is to expound and clarify Scripture but not to apply it, not to rub it into the pores of saints and sinners. That, some would say, is the Holy Spirit's work. But unless one is prepared to say that the Spirit abominates working through human instruments there is no reason he wouldn't be pleased to use not only our work in explaining Scripture but also our sweat in applying Scripture.[2] I've no relish for a debate. I hold that a reader who does not appropriate and/or a teacher who will not apply Scripture is practicing abortion on the Bible. Here is my presupposition on the matter:

> *God has given his word for our instruction and obedience, for our endurance and encouragement; therefore any interpretation that stops short of appropriation is illegitimate.*[3]

Here I intend to discuss deriving application from Old Testament narrative texts. Let's get to it…but let's ease into it slowly.

We begin with a caution: don't assume that application from narrative is obvious.
Narrative is a bit deceptive. Here the text comes in story form. It seems fairly simple and straight-forward. All that remains is to glean an obvious 'lesson' or two out of it. I am not implying that only some hermeneutical high priest can work out proper applications; I am saying that proper application can take more sweat than we may think.

Take 1 Kings 17:2-16. Here Yahweh commands Elijah to go into hiding near the wadi Cherith and assures him that wadi water is for drinking and that ravens will bring him interesting things to eat. Sure enough, Yahweh is as good as his word with those reliable ravens arriving regularly with the prophet's menu. When the wadi dries up, Yahweh directs him to Phoenicia where Elijah finds the Lord's next supplier, a widow an hour away from eating her last supper. As I read I can't help but rejoice in Yahweh's faithfulness in sustaining his servant. And I may suffer no identity crisis at all. I may simply reason that as Elijah is the Lord's servant, so am I (even if Elijah served with more flair), and that Elijah here typifies every believer. Hence what he did for Elijah he will do for me – I can always count on food and drink no matter what. Of course, I will fervently hope the Lord has raised his sanitation standards over the course of redemptive history so that my daily bread will not be raven road-kill. Still, I can be off to Matthew 6:25-34 or Luke 12:22-31 and it's been a swell devotional time.

Perhaps the Spirit cries, 'Whoa!' Why do we think that Elijah typifies every believer? Why do we identify with Elijah here? Who is Elijah? He is the bearer of Yahweh's word – he has the office of prophet (17:1). And his hiding is likely not so much protection from Ahab as a parable to him: when the bearer of Yahweh's word goes into hiding it means Yahweh's word has been hidden from king and people. This withholding of God's word is a token of God's judgment. True, Yahweh sustains his prophet. But why do I so easily identify with Elijah? What about the believing remnant in Israel (cf. 1 Kings 19:18) who cling to Yahweh and yet have no rhythmic ravens making daily deliveries? Why don't I identify myself with those believers who endured the drought and ravages of famine along with the rest of (apostate) Israel and who may have had no special provision from God? Why do I insist on putting myself in the sandals of the office-bearer rather than in those of the remnant?

What then am I saying? That contemporary believers cannot apply 1 Kings 17:2-16 for their own comfort? No, I am only saying that the application may lie in a different direction than we may all too easily suppose. My concern here is not to interpret/apply this text.[4] I only want to underscore that application is not obvious and that it can take a good deal of concentration and perspiration.

I remember my first term in seminary. We had beginning Greek exegesis and were to work in Philippians. That was good, I thought, because I'd already studied it carefully (I thought) – I had preached through the epistle in a college student pastorate. But then came exegesis class. Here is a particular phrase. The prof suggests three possible ways of taking it. That's two more than I'd ever considered. Now once you go through that process a dozen times or so, you can

almost decide to become a biblical agnostic, throw up your
hands, and cry, 'I'll never know what this epistle means!'
Gradually I began to recover from such despair. But, looking
back, I'm pleased I had to wallow through that experience.
I needed it. I needed to come to a point where I began to
think: I'm not sure I know how to interpret the Bible. *Then*
I might make some progress! That is my point here: do not
too easily assume that – well, of course, you know how to
apply this narrative.

'Handles' that can lead to application
I would like to provide some help for the Bible reader or
Bible teacher for moving from narrative to application, or, as
some put it, from preaching to meddling. I'm a bit reluctant
because I don't have a sure-fire, ready-made recipe for doing
so. I can identify a few of what I call 'handles' (or 'pointers')
that one can look for in texts that may lead one to application.
I can label or categorize these 'handles' and discuss them.
But the categories are not air-tight, the list is not exhaustive;
it's only a gimmick meant to give the illusion of organization
while we discuss such things. As long as these caveats are
understood we can proceed.[5]

Procedural
Here I mean that I get a clue for application by analyzing the
procedure that is going on in the text, often a procedure that
the lead character or characters are following. Case in point:
1 Kings 14:1-18, especially verses 1-6.

Royal Relief
Here we find King Jeroboam prepping his wife on how to
approach the old prophet Ahijah. King and Mrs. Jeroboam's
son is ill, likely the heir to the throne. Jeroboam wants to
know if he'll recover and he insists on certain matters likely
to maximize Ahijah's giving them a good word about the
lad. His wife must disguise herself – no imported perfume,

no classy attire; she must look like Mrs. Ordinary Israelite. (Jeroboam needn't have bothered – Ahijah couldn't see anyway). Why was he so concerned the prophet not recognize the royal wife? The text doesn't explicitly say but our guess is all but certain. When Ahijah had originally informed Jeroboam of his coming kingship over ten tribes, he had warned him that he must live a David-like life if he wanted a David-like dynasty (1 Kings 11:38). But Jeroboam got to thinking it over and decided Israel needed its own 'down home' religion in place of the authorized worship in Jerusalem. Hence the bull in Bethel and in Dan (12:25-33). He felt more secure having a religion he could control and a people who weren't cozying up to Jerusalem. He held to this course (13:33-34). So naturally Jeroboam is ill-at-ease about this Ahijah encounter. Ahijah likely views Jeroboam and his religious policy with disdain and will surely answer any query from the king with a scathing denunciation. But if Jeroboam sends his wife, and in disguise, why, Ahijah was much more likely to be compassionate, or at least 'objective.' Who could pronounce a severe word against a dear Israelite mother worried to death over her son? This was likely Jeroboam's thinking. But though Ahijah's sight was shot his hearing was superb, and Yahweh tipped him off about the king's whole scheme (14:4-5). And Ahijah did have a heavy word for her (vv. 7-16).

When we focus on Jeroboam's procedure here, doesn't it open up a path for application (though not the only one from this passage)? Commendably, Jeroboam wants the word of God in his trouble; not so commendably, he has ignored that word throughout his reign. He wants to hear that his son will recover, but he doesn't want to eradicate the bastard worship he has injected into Israel's bloodstream. He wants God's word to alleviate his distress; he does not want it to set his course. He wants that word for his relief but not for his rule; he wants to use but not to follow God's word. He welcomes it as a horoscope to give light on his present dilemma but not as a compass to direct his whole journey. It is a resource he consults, not a regimen to which he submits. He needs its comfort but wants none of its correction. The word of God has become a prostitute – for temporary use only. Once we see this Jeroboam-pattern here we immediately recognize that we see it repeatedly in the course of ministry – one frequently finds people eager for Jesus' aspirin but not interested in his kingship. How often 'Jeroboam' comes to the pastor's study for help. It's even scarier: sometimes the pastor sees the same tendency in his own soul.

Major Mess

Take a look at Genesis 27 – a major fiasco with each human character operating on his/her own principle. We must remember God's previous word in Genesis 25:23 as we come to Genesis 27: 'The older shall serve the younger.'

Immediately we run smack into stubborn Isaac (vv. 1-4). He wants some of Esau's wild game barbecue (cf. 25:28) and then he intends to give Esau his blessing before he dies. Isaac lives by his senses; to be sure, he has no sight (v. 1), so he leans on taste (v. 4), touch (vv. 11, 16, 21-22), smell (vv. 15, 27), and hearing (v. 22). Though he has most of his senses, he has little true sense. Without a doubt he must have known God's clear word to Rebekah in 25:23 (one can't conceive of Rebekah hiding such an urgent and weighty matter from her husband); and yet, here he is flying in the face of it (27:4). By his 'Esau plan' he stands in direct opposition to the clearly given word of God. He will arrange covenant affairs *his* way. It seems so blatant but one can usually rationalize such matters easily enough. In any case, here is Isaac operating by *palate over promise*. He is the patron saint of all who say, 'I don't really care what the word of God says, I must follow my feelings.'

But then eavesdropping Rebekah goes into action (vv. 5-10). Follow Rebekah and watch how *action eclipses faith*. She doesn't diddle around – something had to be *done*. One wonders if Rebekah wasn't a tad irked at the way Isaac went goo-goo over Esau's culinary skills.[6] Why, she could stir up the same stuff with goat meat! Rebekah is the patron saint of all who serve the 'helpless God,' who has no hands but our hands, etc., no schemes but my schemes. She does not bring up the promise issue with Isaac and leave the matter in Yahweh's hands; rather, she seeks to manipulate and deceive. Sometimes our activity may be an expression of faith and sometimes it may be a substitute for faith – and Rebekah's was the latter. We help God out because he is not adequate to care for his own cause. God is a great Promiser, we think, but we cannot trust him to care for and protect his own promise.

There is no 'Mother! That's totally devious!' in Jacob's reactions. He is not shocked by Rebekah's ethics but by the flaws in her plan. He does not say it is wicked but unworkable (vv. 11-12). He has no problem with straight-out, bare-faced lying (vv. 18-19, 24), but one must be careful to be successful at it. His principle is *pragmatism over righteousness*. He was the typical American before there ever was one.

When Rebekah and Jacob's 'successful' scheme comes to light, it blows Isaac's socks off (v. 33) and sends Esau into a pity-filled rage (vv. 34, 36, 38). And before sympathy clouds our reason, we must keep 25:29-34 in mind. Esau had already sold his birthright (and thus his right to the blessing) to Jacob for a mere meal.[7] The writer tells us how we are to assess Esau's sale: 'So Esau despised the birthright' (25:34). We can admit Esau to have been a real man's man – certainly his father's favorite. An outdoorsman par excellence. One imagines him always having a copy of *Field and Stream* sticking out of his back pocket. And one can grant that he was terribly wronged in Jacob's deceiving Isaac. Still, 25:34 gives the bald truth in the matter. It's as if the writer is saying: Don't let the tears (27:38) fool you; he didn't give a rip about the birthright and therefore the blessing; soup mattered more. Pulling this together we can say that *indifference in spite of emotion* characterizes Esau here.

In the summary above I've highlighted the approach of the characters in this episode and, hopefully, in each case you can see a 'handle' for moving toward application. However, in this text (and the text rules, doesn't it?) we must not become so enamored with the human characters that we miss the big point.[8] Where are we left at the end of Genesis 27? With four sinners – and all of them in the wrong, all of them misusing or abusing Yahweh's promise (25:23) in some way. Did Yahweh approve of Rebekah and Jacob's shenanigans since they were both pro-promise? No. Nor of Isaac's thick-headed resistance to it. But Yahweh's promise *did* come to pass. So the text teaches us that Yahweh's promise will prove true in spite of *all* efforts to sabotage it. In spite of the network of 'free' and sinful wills opposing or 'aiding' his decision, God brings his word to pass – if not through man's consent then in the face of his resistance, if not through man's cooperation then through and in spite of his rebellion. What hope and help that should give his people! It can be useful to trace the procedure of characters in a narrative and thereby to find pointers for application; but it's wrong to be so taken with those items that we turn our eyes off the invincible God the text reveals.

Conceptual

Some narrative texts want to make us think or change the way we think; they want, as we say, to play with our mind. Hence some texts lend themselves to what I would call a conceptual application. We are not too keen on this these days; we would rather textual applications move our emotions or explain our duty. We may think all of application involves either soothing our feelings or directing our behavior, not renewing our mind. But often a biblical narrative wants to get us to change our thinking or adopt its perspective on matters. Several examples...

The worst of times

Take a look at 1 Kings 16:29-17:1. The writer introduces Ahab, Israel's new king – and the new paganism he brings in with him. Jeroboam had already spread a pallor of death over Israel with his bull-calf worship (12:25-33), but Ahab was giving her the lethal injection of Baal worship. The writer pounds this peril into us as he tells us that Ahab married Jezebel, the daughter of Eth*baal*, that he served *Baal*, erected an altar to *Baal,* and built a temple of *Baal* (16:31-32). Just like that. Nothing to stop him. Then:

> Elijah the Tishbite from the sojourners in Gilead said to Ahab, 'By the life of Yahweh the God of Israel, before whom I stand, there will not be dew or rain these years except by my word' (1 Kings 17:1).

Ronald Wallace has captured this moment so well that I quote him at length:

> Elijah appears on the scene with startling suddenness. Indeed, his appearance is a mystery. We want to know more about this man when we suddenly see him stand before the king. We want to know where he came from, and where he was trained in the things of God. We want to know how he received his call to be a prophet to his time. But we know as little about him as Ahab knew about him, and it is better so. For to see him appear thus reminds us that we need not despair when we see great movements of evil achieving spectacular success on this earth, for we may be sure that God, in unexpected places, has already secretly prepared His counter-movement....Therefore the situation is never hopeless where God is concerned. Whenever evil flourishes, it is always a superficial flourish, for at the height of the triumph of evil God will be there, ready with His man and His movement and His plans to ensure that His own cause will never fail.[9]

I think Wallace nicely grabs hold of the way the text wants us to *think*. Here is swaggering, domineering, government-sponsored paganism carrying the day in Israel. Out of nowhere Elijah appears. He so much as asks if Ahab has his fertility worship all ready to go and then declares that Yahweh has decided to cancel fertility until further notice. Then he disappears (vv. 2-3). The suddenness and strangeness of the text are meant to affect the way we look at such times – and at such a God.

Dwight Eisenhower had risen to commander of all the Allied forces in Europe during World War II. Riding a crest of post-war popularity he was elected president of the United States in 1952. Having been in 'higher' positions for some time Eisenhower had grown accustomed to lesser details being handled by 'lesser lights' around him. During his presidency, he even had someone dress him. His valet, John Moaney, would put Eisenhower's watch on him while Ike held out his wrist. He would pull up Ike's boxer shorts. But the lifestyle backfired. After he left public office, Ike was almost totally ignorant of how to pay for things at a department store, adjust a TV set, get past a tollbooth on the highway – or even to dial a phone![10] There he was, at the top, but practically helpless, unprepared for life where it is lived.

I think we can construct a graven image of God like that. We can say all the orthodox things about God but wonder if he is caught unprepared in the emergencies of his people. We wouldn't question that Yahweh is mighty, we simply wonder sometimes if he is competent. Sometimes we can nearly get sucked into the 'helpless god' syndrome (HGS), as if we have a Dagon on our hands (1 Sam. 5:1-5). So we need mind-correcting texts like 1 Kings 17:1. We need to see afresh that when evil has its heyday and comes steamrolling over the people of God, he is not caught unprepared. Elijah's epiphany reminds us that 'God, in unexpected places, has already secretly prepared his counter-movement' and that 'at the height of the triumph of evil God will be there.'

Hills-and-plains theology

There is a section of 1 Kings 20, verses 23-30 to be exact, that almost grabs a reader by the shirt and says, 'Well, how *do* you

think about God?' Let's back up and get a running start at
this chunk of narrative.

Ben-hadad (probably II) and the Syrians had suffered a
disastrous reverse in battle at the hands of Israel (vv. 13-21)
and the king's military advisors were advocating a revised
plan in order to recoup Syrian honor. There were two
problems with their previous engagement with Israel.
(Actually, three: alcohol for lunch proved a poor choice,
v. 16). One was strategy (vv. 24-25), the other theology (v. 23).
The latter is rather heartening to hear, for it's hard to find
military personnel willing to talk theology:

> Their gods are gods of the hills – that's why they were stronger
> than we; however, let's fight with them on level ground –
> surely we will prove stronger than they (v. 23).

And Ben-hadad took their advice. At war season next year
the Syrians chose their ground at the Aphek east of the Sea of
Chinnereth/Galilee. But Syria's theology drew heaven's fire
– a prophet comes to Ahab of Israel with an assuring word:

> Here's what Yahweh says: 'Because Aram [Syria] has said,
> "Yahweh is a god of the hills and not a god of the valleys,"
> I shall give all this vast army into your hand, and you [plural]
> shall know that I am Yahweh' (v. 28).

The rub in this section of the narrative centers on this
fallacious Syrian theology – on their erroneous way of
thinking about Yahweh (a conceptual matter). I should
think a faithful reader would ask, 'How do *I* think wrongly
about God? Have I in some way sucked up a dose of Syrian
thinking?' That would be, I would hold, a proper beginning.

But only a beginning. And here is a tricky bit about
application: we must see that, in this case at least, our Syrian-
like theology will probably not take the exact form as that
of Ben-hadad's generals. It is easy to look at 1 Kings 20:23
and say, 'Stupid pagans! But that's the way those dolts
thought back then.'[11] But to let the text get uncomfortably

close to yourself (and to others) you have to engage in a
bit of hard thinking about this Syrian thinking. Being a
more sophisticated sinner than a Syrian, I must ask how
I provincialize Yahweh's power, though in a different form.
Perhaps I have no trouble believing that God rules the affairs
of nations but can't conceive he could have any interest in my
oncology appointment this afternoon. Or reverse it. Perhaps
you have no difficulty casting the details of life (cf. 2 Kings 6:5)
before the Lord but you have next to no sense of a God who
orders and directs the military campaigns and foreign affairs
of nations (cf. 2 Kings 5:1). It's the 'God-is-this-but-not-
that' syndrome. Or you look back on the package of despair
you used to call your life. Perhaps a sad childhood with
little parental affection, early and stupid choices, twisted
relationships that have scarred and deadened. And you think
Jesus Christ may be a mighty Savior for folks of a 'normal'
stripe, who had a little help from parents and/or church,
and who haven't wallowed in their own moral labyrinth and
turned into walking basket cases. But a creep like you? No,
Jesus is only a Savior on the hills, not down in the valleys and
pits where you are. You have a Syrian mind.

I shan't go on with this. I simply want to insist that seeing
an 'application handle' in the text may be only the starting-
point for application. One must translate in this case the
Syrian mind-set into the forms in which *we* display it.
And how do we do that? 'Look into your own sinful heart.'
Alexander Whyte rides again!

You will find gobs of texts that want to play with your
mind. Their application has primarily to do with your
thinking – they may want to anchor or reinforce your
thinking, to change your thinking, or at least to stir it. Ask
yourself why the story of sparing a pagan Canaanite harlot
is told in Joshua 2. Is it there to at least stimulate your
thinking? What about Joshua 11:6-7, where in back-to-back
verses divine sovereignty and human ingenuity are stacked
side-by-side? Does the Holy Spirit expect your mind simply

to slide over that with nary a notice or scarcely a thought? Doesn't the story of Judges 9 intend to make you think about the quietness (and certainty) of divine judgment?[12]

Situational

Often the circumstances a narrative character or characters face may prove a handle for application. Not what the character is doing but what he/she is facing may prove a bridge to our contemporary hearers.

The trouble with 'After these things...'

Take the clip in 1 Kings 17:17-24, which tells of the widow of Zarephath's troubles.[13] Note especially verses 17-18 – her boy becomes sick and dies. Nothing unusual about that. Happened all the time – no antibiotics. Sad, to be sure. But verses 8-16 lend some color to her trouble. There she was preparing for their last supper because of a severe famine. Elijah had requested a first installment of that meal for himself (vv. 11-13). He gave her the incentive of Yahweh's promise that her flour and oil would never run out until the rains returned (v. 14). She walked in the obedience of faith and found there was always enough for pancakes (vv. 15-16). Yahweh proved her faithful sustainer. Then her son sickens and dies. It's as much a theological problem as an emotional distress. Has Yahweh, the God of Israel who has preserved their lives, suddenly reversed himself? When all the tests are in, is Yahweh just as flaky and capricious as the pagan gods?

But consider simply the transition from verses 8-16 to verses 17-18. This widow goes from the victory of faith to the valley of sorrow. The next paragraph of life can slam you flat on the ground. And one wonders what the God of Israel is doing. Is this not a well-worn experience of many of the Lord's people? The sunshine of his goodness suddenly becomes the slime of the pit; his mysterious providence comes hard on the heels of his marvelous providence. Now I think (though others may think I'm off the wall and out of the park here) a preacher should point out this rub – or sequence – in the text. Quite a number of a pastor's congregation would gather immense comfort from simply seeing the widow's dilemma. They would say to themselves, 'Yes, that's exactly the sort of thing I'm facing just now – I have had these obvious and distinct evidences of the goodness of the Lord and now he seems to have body-slammed me to the mat.' And a preacher need not solve this problem; his people will get much encouragement if he simply identifies it in the text. They will get the sense that the Bible is a book that *understands* them. And they will have assurance that their own experience is not whacky or weird but fits one of the biblical patterns of God's strange way with his people.

Some qualifications. I know this is not the only point in the passage, that 1 Kings 17:17-24 has more teaching and more applications than this one. I also know (or at least I think) that the primary concern of the passage is for the honor of Yahweh, and I must not allow the need of the widow to eclipse that.[14] Yet it's not primarily a matter of the widow's need but of God's ways. 'Now it came about after these things…' (v. 17a). The everlasting jar of flour is followed by the devastating death of her son. This can happen: the storm can cover the sun and leave life in bits and pieces. Many of God's people know this God – the God who both sustains and bewilders, the One who lifts up and dashes down, the One who places you under the smile of his grace and then suddenly disappears into the darkness. And they find strange but incredible comfort when someone assures them from the text that this is a biblical and not atypical experience.[15]

Elisha the Great?
Please look at 2 Kings 4:8-37, and especially at verses 25b-37. This woman from Shunem has also just gotten whacked in the solar plexus of life: the son Elisha had promised her had been born, but, after a few short years, died (vv. 18-20). She hurries

on her way to find the prophet. When she reaches him at Mt. Carmel, she throws decorum to the winds, seizes Elisha by the feet, and lets go her anguish (vv. 26-27a). Gehazi, Elisha's servant, is about to push her away and restore order. Elisha stops him with: 'Let her alone, for she is in bitter distress, and Yahweh [emphatic] has hidden it from me and has not told me' (v. 27b). Elisha directs Gehazi to run back to Shunem and place Elisha's staff on the dead boy (v. 29). Orders executed but no change (v. 31). So when Elisha arrives his only recourse is prayer, begging Yahweh to restore life (v. 33).

The text depicts Elisha as limited in both wisdom (v. 27) and power (vv. 31, 33). The prophet's situation here is, I think, a launching pad for application. And application may take two directions. It could go the way of contrast. Here is Elisha in his office as prophet, laboring under all the limitations he has (through no fault of his own). But there is no such inadequacy in Jesus our prophet par excellence. He is not left in the dark (cf. John 5:20) and, in the face of death, he is not reduced to prayer but *speaks* the dead to life (Luke 7:14-15). The limitations of Elisha point to the sufficiency of Jesus. We could go that way in application.

We could also focus on Elisha's situation as analogous to ours. We are not prophets like Elisha was. (At least I'm not – I don't receive direct divine revelation as he did). But simply in our non-technical position as the Lord's servants, don't we know something of the same limitations? Aren't there scores of times when folks seek us out for advice in their dilemmas, and we have to so much as say, 'The Lord has hidden it from me and has not told me'? I hate being so deficient in wisdom, so baffled about what to make of people's twisted problems, but Elisha's situation is a comfort to me. Does it not suggest that I don't have to give 'the answer' to everyone's perplexity? I don't have to take on the impossible burden of playing God and tell people what 'God is doing' or 'saying' in their trouble. God has not called me – nor gifted me – to have the solution for everyone's quandaries. What a relief it is finally to realize that. What a weight it lifts from ministry! In fact, we get in trouble when we fail to see our limitations.

Paul Tripp tells of a family episode when his children were young. One son was playing 'baseball' in the back yard by hitting stones with a rake handle. His three-year-old brother was wandering around the yard and, after while, happened to get in the path of one of those hard projectiles accelerated by his brother's rake handle. It smacked him in the forehead. It was in no way deliberate. Still…profuse bleeding. All went into emergency mode. Paul wiped away the blood to see the extent of the injury. His little son, Darnay, lay quietly and seemingly at peace. Paul noticed his lips were moving, so he got down near Darnay's mouth to hear. He heard him saying, over and over, 'I'm just so glad my daddy is a doctor!' The child knew his father had a 'Dr.' in front of his name and that he sometimes had appointments with people.[16] But Ph.D.s are not much use if one has a head injury. He had no clue of his father's limitations.

And in ministry we can be dangerous if we cannot see our own limitations. Like Elisha, where is the shame in admitting the Lord has not given us light on a matter and that we are reduced to begging him in prayer? Don't think I am advocating being wishy-washy and never having biblical answers to give. I am working on a different front. Those who hold a high view of the Bible's authority sometimes hold a high view of their own ability to assess people's circumstances and to prescribe solutions. Sometimes this is sheer arrogance, and they'd do better to ask themselves if perhaps, for once, the Lord has hidden it from them.

Judicial

Sometimes the biblical writer will make a judgment about or an assessment of a character or event and we readers are expected to acquiesce in that appraisal. Granted, often it can be difficult to capture the narrator's point of view, because narrative tends by nature to be more descriptive than didactic, more indirect than overt, more subtle than obvious. However, when the narrative writer does make a judgment we are intended to submit to it, and – I would claim – that judgment may prove another fruitful 'handle' for application. I am using the term 'judicial' in a general sense to suggest assessment, not to conjure up courtroom images.

Occasionally, a writer's direct judgment on a matter gives us the proper point of view, which needs to come before application anyway. How helpful is the last line of Genesis 25:34: 'So Esau despised the birthright.' That gives us some real help in looking at the episode in 25:27-34. He does not say Jacob was a slimy opportunist but that Esau did not give a rip about covenantal matters. This then helps us when we view Esau's rage and grief and work through application in Genesis 27.

Better yet bad

Let's look at an easily ignored piece of text: 2 Kings 3:1-3. It's simply the introductory comment to the reign of Jehoram of Israel. We're so accustomed by now (were we reading straight through 1–2 Kings, that is) to negative assessments of northern kings that we don't bat an eye as we read 'He did evil in Yahweh's eyes' (v. 2a). But suddenly we are told that his evil has a unique element: it is not as evil an evil as Ahab and Jezebel's evil (v. 2b); Jehoram removed – at least for the time being – the 'pillar of Baal.' But the writer is unimpressed, as he says in verse 3: 'Nevertheless, he clung to the sins of Jeroboam the son of Nebat...he did not depart from them.' Jehoram may go lighter on severe sin but presses on in standard sin. Just because Jeroboam's perversion was government-funded and long-practiced (see 1 Kings 12:25-33) doesn't shave away the writer's intolerance. So the Kings' writer is saying Jehoram was not as bad as he could have been and yet he was not righteous as he should have been. The writer seems bitten by a holy intolerance; putting some wraps on Baal worship while clinging to Jeroboam's calves is not how one loves Yahweh with all one's heart, soul, and being. What is it about Commandments One and Two that Jehoram doesn't understand?

John Feinstein has written a book called *A Civil War*. It's about the rivalry of what in my country is called 'college football,' and especially about the 1995 football season of the Naval Academy in Annapolis, Maryland, and that of the Cadets of 'Army' in West Point (New York). He tells of the game that year between Army and nearly-perennial power Notre Dame. Notre Dame was off to an early lead, but then an out-classed Army team tightened up, began to do some of their own scoring. Suffice to say Army scored a touchdown at almost the end of the game. This made the score 28-27, Notre Dame in the lead by one point. By football rules, Army had a decision to make after this touchdown. They could go for an 'extra point,' done by kicking the ball through the goal post – almost always a sure thing – so getting one point and playing Notre Dame to a 28-28 tie (now they play overtime which eliminates such ties). Or…they had the option of going for two points, which meant they had to run or pass the ball from three yards out into the end zone. That's tougher to do, but, if Army did so, they would win by one point, 29-28. What to do? Go for a sure one, tie Notre Dame, suck the air out of Notre Dame's balloon, and put a blotch on her vaunted reputation? Or go for two, go for the win, knowing that if it failed, Army would lose? The choice was not hard really. Coach Sutton and the Amry players had not come to play Notre Dame to a tie. They came to win. They went for two. And failed. Army lost 28-27. But one admires that. A lost game but a right decision. One doesn't play football games to tie but to win. And when there is the possibility of winning one should go all-out to win.

The writer of 2 Kings would, I think, understand. He does not rest content by saying, 'Well, now we have Jehoram, and he is wicked, but it's a more moderate wickedness than Ahab, so we should be rather pleased.' 'He is not really righteous at all, but he's a tad closer to righteous than Ahab.' 'Nevertheless, he clung to the sins of Jeroboam.' One senses a kind of livid discontent behind that 'Nevertheless.' Who can be satisfied with that?, he says. That's not what Deuteronomy 6:5 demands, he would say. We are baffled when the God who wants one holy passion is not delighted with a few puny substitutes. As I have written elsewhere, 'This impatience of the Bible that refuses to accept anything less than total fidelity is only a reflection of the intolerant God of the Bible who insists on having all your affections.'[17]

All of this does not work out the application in detail. It may need fleshed out in specific examples. But hopefully the direction of application is clear – and it begins by picking up on a judgment the biblical writer makes and following it through.

God-speak

Calvin Coolidge, US president during most of the 1920s, was legendary for his silence and verbal paucity. There is a story about Coolidge when he was Vice-President: a woman next to him at a dinner party claimed he simply must talk to her because she had made a bet earlier that day that she could get more than two words out of him. Coolidge turned to her and mathematically replied, 'You lose.' Now generally biblical narrators are a lot like Coolidge – reticent to talk, i.e., they don't come right out and tell the reader what they think but tell the story and allow the reader to divine what they think. But, as noted, there are times when the narrator gives a candid, direct assessment. And, when he does, we should pay attention since it may lead us to fruitful application. How much more when God himself speaks in a narrative text!

Take Job 42:7-8, for example:

(7) After Yahweh had spoken these words to Job, Yahweh said to Eliphaz the Temanite, 'My anger burns against you and

your two friends, for you have not spoken about me what is right as my servant Job has. (8) And now take for yourselves seven bulls and seven rams and go to my servant Job, and you shall offer up a burnt-offering for yourselves, and *Job my servant* will pray for you. Surely I will accept him, so as not to deal out disgrace to you, for you have not spoken about me what is right as my servant Job has.'

Of course, most of Job is not narrative, but it is wrapped with narrative (chs. 1–2 and 42:7-17). And here, in the closing narrative section, is Yahweh's ironic vindication of Job: 'my servant Job,' he calls him; he regards him just as he had in 1:8 and 2:3. In 42:8b 'Job my servant' is emphatic, which underscores the irony: Job the sinner (in the friends' view) must be Job the intercessor (in Yahweh's view).

It is striking that Yahweh says that Job had spoken 'what is right' (or, 'firm') about Yahweh. I cannot agree with Dillard and Longman that Yahweh's 'what is right' refers only to Job's 'repentance' in 42:5-6.[18] All of the friends' words – and therefore all of Job's – are in view. Ellison then is surely on target:

> The force of 42:7 is that however foolishly he may have said it, Job was looking for a God big enough to comprehend his experience. On the other hand, however wisely they may have put it into words, his friends were upholding a God small enough to conform to their theories.[19]

So Job's right speaking includes 3:11-12, 20, 23; and 7:19-21; and 30:19-21, for example. All his despair, anguish, accusation, and terror. And, according to Yahweh, Eliphaz & Co. did not speak what is right about him. They made many true statements about God – a lot of their systematic theology was on target.[20] Much of it was well-sculpted and beautifully said. But Yahweh insists, 'You have not spoken about me what is right.'

Had we read clear through the book we could have observed that the friends are always talking *about* God. Job does that too and yet he keeps turning *to* God at the same time (perhaps partly out of frustration with his friends). In any case, Job keeps turning from his friends and speaking to God (note 7:7-21 ['Remember' in v. 7 is an imperative *singular* – hence he turns to God here]; 9:28-31; and 10:2-22).[21] Bonhoeffer has, incidentally, warned us that the Fall involved a religious, theological conversation *about* God.[22]

Here then is Yahweh's assessment of the friends' work – they had 'not spoken what is right' about him. Is not such an assessment the sobering word that ought to drive us into a process of personal application? Ought not this text be hanging on the wall of pastors' studies haunting us continually? Ought not this statement come crashing upon the conscience of every worshiper preparing to speak of and to God in public or private worship? How easily we blabber along scarcely thinking that words are weighed. What care this demands of a pastor – that week-by-week he not distort or trivialize or pervert what is true about God.

Peggy Noonan tells about the day in March 1981 when Ronald Reagan was shot and was rushed to the ER at George Washington University Hospital. No one knew how badly he was hurt although he had been coughing up blood on the way. When they arrived at the walkway, Reagan pulled himself out of the limo on his own. He then stood up straight, sucked in his mid-section, hitched up his trousers, and buttoned his suit jacket. It was vintage Reagan – getting himself together; one must 'do it right' even when entering an emergency room. And he did, till he crumbled after going about thirty feet.[23]

That attitude must sink into our pores when we speak about God: this must be done properly; we must take care to care about this. Are the times not legion when we need the ministry of intercession and atonement for our teaching and theologizing (vv. 8-9)? When we must bring our preaching and our worship and our theological discussions to the cross of Jesus and have them washed from their perversion and flippancy? Doesn't Yahweh here expose the ongoing need of every theologian – that he must stand under atonement and prayer?

Let's include one more 'handle' for application and call it the...

Doxological

Frequently narratives drive us to what I would call a 'dox-ological' application – they simply want us to respond with praise. It's important to keep this always in mind because there is such a tendency when we think of 'application' to focus on human needs or 'my' difficulties. Since I plan to elaborate on this matter in the next chapter, let me give but one example of 'doxological' application.

We can focus on 2 Kings 4:8-17, part of the story of Elisha and the Shunammite woman. The prophet wants to reward her for her kindness to him and, after his servant Gehazi does a background check on her circumstances, promises her that she will have a son (vv. 14-16a). She finds even the thought incredible (v. 16b) and yet the fulfillment very factual (v. 17).

Now it helps to do a little leg work with the text: (1) to note that the phrase 'at the time of reviving' (lit.) in verses 16 and 17 only occurs elsewhere in Genesis 18:10 and 14, where Sarah struggles with swallowing the Lord's promise of a son; (2) which brings to mind the whole barren-woman pattern and conjures up Sarah (Gen. 11:30ff.), Rebekah (Gen. 25), Rachel (Gen. 29–30), Manoah's wife (Judg. 13), perhaps Ruth (Ruth, 1, 4), Hannah (1 Sam. 1), and Elizabeth (Luke 1); (3) and yet with a bit of reflection we see this 2 Kings 4 situation is unique among all of these others – the child of all these mothers was either to be a great leader/helper/deliverer for Israel or was absolutely essential in carrying on even a biological covenant line. This 2 Kings 4 lad doesn't have a name, was not vital to Israel's very existence, nor did he ever, so far as we know, do anything more outstanding than carry on the family farm. All of which cranks up the Doxology. Why did God then give this woman a son? Apparently because he wanted to make her happy with a child. Sometimes it is as simple as that. God must get pleasure when he makes his people happy – no wonder he does so much of it. Isn't the text tugging at your knees, that is, to get you into a position for adoration? How so? Why, simply because here is a God who delights to 'give good gifts' (Matt. 7:11) to his people, not because such gifts will prove of great use to him but because they will give his people joy. Sometimes that's the only 'application' a biblical text wants to make – to get you to fall on your face and adore the God it depicts. Sometimes it's as simple as that.

We end with another caution – don't claim too much from narrative

It's one spine-tingling, antacid episode: that story of 1 Samuel 26. There David and Abishai are standing near or over a sleeping Saul and debating what to do with him. Both are talking theology. Abishai claims it's obvious that God has handed Saul over to David's clutches and he (Abishai) is perfectly eager to prove himself God's efficient servant (v. 8). David himself is no slouch at theology and appeals to principle (v. 9), providence (v. 10), and conscience (v. 11a). Since David's the boss, they pilfer Saul's canteen and spear and hightail it out of camp (vv. 11b-12a). Only then are we told *why* neither Saul nor any of his crack troops awoke (v. 12b – a deep sleep from Yahweh).

Then there is that delectable scene when David gets to a safe distance (v. 13). He startles army-career man Abner awake and rails at him and the rest for shoddy sentry duty (v. 15). No doubt about the executions army 'regs' should impose for such dereliction (v. 16a). David is not 'storying' to them – he has the king's spear and canteen (v. 16b)!

When we consider what application(s) we should make from this story we implicitly sense (I hope) that the narrative does not indicate that God will help me play neat tricks on my enemy. In fact, when I think it out, the story does not allow me to claim any of David's benefits here as necessarily mine. Did God marvelously protect David from danger here? Certainly. Does that mean he will always do that for me? No. Maybe my 'Saul' (I dislike speaking this way, but you can catch the drift) will get me. Or cancer. Or a tornado. Or a traffic accident in a Wal-Mart parking lot (which, by the way, is more dangerous than the highway).

So I must ask: Why is David being given such superb, if nail-biting, protection here? Because Yahweh had ordained that David would be king of Israel in Saul's place and so Yahweh will see that he is preserved for that office. That means that David is, in 'redemptive-historical' terms, more important than I am. Or than you are. If that makes you upset, file a suit through your local Civil Liberties Union. But God has appointed David to a special office of leadership over his people and, by one way or another, he must be preserved to fulfill that destiny. I am not saying that God does not care for me or that he does not have an ordained plan for my life; I am only saying I do not hold a crucial place (like David) in God's bringing his kingdom into this world. Hence I cannot make the assumption from 1 Samuel 26 that I will be infallibly protected as David was.

In fact, this is often the wrong track. I mean this tendency to have to identify with a biblical character. I realize it is a natural tendency but it frequently places the emphasis where it shouldn't be (at least not initially). But what if I lift my eyes to Yahweh and ask what *he* is doing in 1 Samuel 26? Then I see that he is, among other things, encouraging his tattered servant David. The fact that Abishai and David stood unmolested by Saul in the middle of the king's camp, that Saul was utterly defenseless, that, had they chosen, they could have liquidated him, that they carted off the 'sacrament' of Saul's position (his spear) – all of this must have tremendously heartened David. It was clearly a sign for David: Saul's power is gone; nothing can keep David from obtaining the kingdom.

Does this mean 1 Samuel 26 has no application to my case? Not at all. If I place my eyes on Yahweh here, I see him as the God who gives tokens of encouragement to his desperate servant. Granted, I may not have the redemptive-historical 'importance' of David, but, if through the crucified and risen One I know David's God, will he not likely prove to be the same sort of God to me? You may prefer something better, but I am just as content with Yahweh's *tendencies* as with his promises. It is simply 'vintage Yahweh' to stoop down into his servants' nasty circumstances and put fresh heart into them.

I remember one of those 'gospel' songs that I sometimes heard when I was very young: 'It is no secret what God can do / what he's done for others / he'll do for you.' It's a rhythmic jingle but a poor hermeneutical principle, simply because what he's done for others he may not do for you. But 1 Samuel 26, I think, encourages us to say that what he *is* for others, he'll be for you. It's not as precise but should be enough. In terms of 1 Samuel 26, it means that David's situation does not so much control our application of the text as the character of David's God. That's where one always finds treasure.

Endnotes

1. G. F. Barbour, *The Life of Alexander Whyte, D.D.* (London: Hodder and Stoughton, 1923), 307-308.

2. Cf. Westminster Confession of Faith, 5/3: 'God in his ordinary providence *maketh use of means*, yet is free to work without, above, and against them, at his pleasure' (emphasis mine).

3. For the record I've found there are two basic types of application – encouragement or exposure, or, what is the same, consolation or criticism. The cliché seems to be correct: Scripture intends to comfort the afflicted and afflict the comfortable.

4. On 1 Kings 17:2-16 see M. B. Van't Veer, *My God is Yahweh* (St. Catharines, Ont.: Paideia, 1980), 73-79; or see my summary in *The Wisdom and the Folly: An Exposition of the Book of First Kings* (Ross-shire: Christian Focus, 2002), 207-213.

5. For decent detail on these matters, see Richard L. Pratt, Jr., *He Gave Us Stories* (Brentwood, TN: Wolgemuth and Hyatt, 1990), 307-402 (= Part 3, Applying Old Testament Narratives), and Daniel M. Doriani, *Putting the Truth to Work: The Theory and Practice of Biblical Application* (Phillipsburg, NJ: Presbyterian & Reformed, 2001).

6. Cf. Derek Kidner, *Genesis*, Tyndale Old Testament Commentaries (London: Tyndale, 1967), 156.

7. See John D. Currid, *A Study Commentary on Genesis*, 2 vols. (Darlington: Evangelical Press, 2003), 2:21; and Bruce K. Waltke, *Genesis: A Commentary* (Grand Rapids: Zondervan, 2001), 363-64.

8. See S. G. DeGraaf, *Promise and Deliverance*, 4 vols. (St. Catharines, Ont.: Paideia, 1977), 1:187.

9. Ronald S. Wallace, *Elijah and Elisha* (Grand Rapids: Eerdmans, 1957), 3.

10. Cormac O'Brien, *Secret Lives of the U. S. Presidents* (Philadelphia: Quirk Books, 2004), 203.

11. This is a critical point in application, for we are perverse and often love to escape the point of a text. We can do this by *archaizing* the text (i.e., 'Those pagans were stupid to think of Yahweh like that, but, of course, being orthodox believers, we are never thick like that') or by *generalizing* it (e.g., 'Well, we all likely do that sort of thing at one time or another'), and so failing to make particular and pointed application.

12. On this cf. my *Judges: Such a Great Salvation* (Ross-shire: Christian Focus, 2000), 127.

13. Contrary to some critics, I take the woman of verses 17-24 to be identical with the one of verses 8-16; see *The Wisdom and the Folly*, 219-21.

14. One must always be on guard against a human need or condition in a passage controlling the interpretation of that text. First Kings 19 is a case in point: so many readers and interpreters are so sure Elijah is wiped out by some combination of pride, fear, self-pity, and depression that they seem immune to the text and refuse to take Elijah's own assertions as bearing more than a semblance of truth. For my own effort in opposition, cf. the chapter 'Shall the Psychotherapists Win?' in *The Wisdom and the Folly* (1 Kings), 257-75.

15. Cf. a somewhat similar sequence in David's experience in 1 Samuel 30:1-6; he has just been marvelously kept from having to fight with the Philistines against Israel (1 Sam. 29) – and then arrives at Ziklag to find it burned and the women and children taken captive.

16. Paul David Tripp, *Instruments in the Redeemer's Hands* (Phillipsburg, NJ: Presbyterian & Reformed, 2002), 42-43.

17. *2 Kings: The Power and the Fury* (Ross-shire: Christian Focus, 2005), 43.

18. Raymond B. Dillard and Tremper Longman III, *An Introduction to the Old Testament* (Grand Rapids: Zondervan, 1994), 208. In fact, 'repentance' hardly fits 42:6 rightly translated. For one thing, the first verb has been skewed by making it reflexive – 'despise myself' (RSV, NIV, ESV). The Hebrew verb is *not* reflexive; there is no 'myself' there. It is the translators' guess, and not a particularly good one. The verb is simply 'I retract/reject/despise.' But *what* is retracted or rejected is not stated. There are two contextual possibilities: Job rejects his words that had gone over the top (see 42:3; so JB, NLT), or Job rejects his previous, deficient, second-hand knowledge of Yahweh (42:5, 'I had heard of you by the hearing of the ear, but now...'). I think the latter is preferable.

The second verb, usually translated 'repent,' is *nācham*. If it is translated 'repent,' what kind of 'repentance' is meant? It can hardly denote repentance for sin, since Yahweh has not accused Job of particular sin (though note 40:1-2, 6-8). Indeed, he vindicates him in 42:7 as having spoken 'what is right' about him. *Nācham* is often used of God repenting (or not repenting, as the case may be). It is so used about 25 times. In such cases it means to *relent*, to reverse one's judgment or projected course of action. Job could have 'repented' in such a way, meaning: 'I reverse my judgment, I withdraw my demand; there is no more reason to argue my case with you, for you, Yahweh, have shown that you are *for* me.' But *nācham* also carries the meaning 'to comfort/console oneself,' and that is likely the meaning here. A form of this verb is used in 2:11, where Job's friends come to 'comfort him.' What the friends failed to do, Yahweh did, so that Job says, 'I comfort myself upon dust and ashes.' But someone will object, 'No, it still must mean "repent (of sin)", because it says that he did it "in dust and ashes" and dust and ashes signify mourning and penitence.' But the dust and ashes here signify the town dump, the mound where Job was sitting. If 'dust and ashes' signifies anything, it signifies Job's isolation. Moreover, '*in* dust and ashes' is a poor rendering of the Hebrew, which is more properly '*upon* dust and ashes.' The dust and ashes have nothing to do with Job's attitude but with his *location*. There would not be much point in Job's saying he repents on the city dump, but it would be quite gripping for him to say he comforted himself – in light of Yahweh's coming to him – on that place of isolation and separation.

Translate then: 'Therefore I reject [my former, second-hand knowledge of you] and I comfort myself upon dust and ashes.'

This translation obviously affects how one looks at the whole book. I think it shows the grand consistency of the work. I owe big thanks to Dr. G. Douglas Young for first suggesting this alternative understanding in OT Poets class at Trinity Evangelical Divinity School.

19. H. L. Ellison, *From Tragedy to Triumph* (Grand Rapids: Eerdmans, 1958), 126-27. This leads Genung (in the old edition of ISBE, 3:1685) to exclaim: 'Job's honest and immensely revelatory words, anger, remonstrance, bold arraignment of God's way and all, were "the thing that is right." There is no more tremendous Divine pronouncement in all Scripture than this.' Cf. also Robert Fyall's discussion in his superb *How Does God Treat His Friends?* (Ross-shire: Christian Focus, 1995), 135-38.

20. Still, it gives me the 'willies' every time I see a quote on a church letterhead or in a church bulletin taken (with apparent approval) from Eliphaz, Bildad, Zophar – or Elihu.

21. 'It is important to notice that Job does not speak of God without at the same time looking up to Him as in prayer. Although he feels rejected by God, he still remains true to God' (Franz Delitzsch, *Biblical Commentary on the Book of Job*, 2 vols. [1872; reprint ed., Grand Rapids: Eerdmans, 1949], 1:160). Cf. F. I. Andersen: 'His prayers may shock his religious friends, but at least he keeps on talking to the heedless God. His friends talk about God. Job talks to God. And this makes him the only authentic theologian in the book' (*Job*, Tyndale Old Testament Commentaries [Downers Grove: Inter-Varsity, 1976], 98).

22. D. Bonhoeffer, *Creation and Fall/Temptation* (New York: Macmillan, 1967), 69.

23. *When Character Was King* (New York: Viking, 2001), 170-71.

CHAPTER 8

Center

There is an amusing sentence in one of Walker Percy's novels. He describes Lewis Peckham, a self-appointed golf pro: 'There was a space in him where a space shouldn't be, where parts were not glued together.'[1] Whatever might be the case of fictional Lewis, that should not be true of our biblical interpretation – it should be pulled together, integrated, have a proper focus. Hence, for my money, here is the premier presupposition that should undergird all our biblical interpretation:

> *God has given his word as a revelation of himself; if then I use his word rightly, I will long to see him, and he will be the focus of my study.*

And so we must read Old Testament narrative with a *theocentric* focus. In all our reading we should keep our eye on God – what he is revealing about himself and how he is working.[2] We should feast our eyes on the triune God. Some may immediately object: Don't we need to start at the other end? Don't we need to begin with the needs of people? Shouldn't we be 'existential' before we get 'theological'? Must we not ensure that our biblical study is relevant? I don't even care to argue. I will only assert: if you keep your eye on God you *will* address the needs of (his) people. It happens in the process. And my way is far more interesting, because there is no one so disturbing, so surprising, so steadying, so fascinating as the God of the Bible. So if I had one piece of hermeneutical advice to give it is: keep your focus on God if you want your biblical interpretation to be accurate, interesting, nourishing, and relevant.

What then do we need to keep 'on center' in our interpretation of Old Testament narratives?

A Constant Perspective

By this I simply mean, as already stated, that we must adopt a discipline of always looking at our texts from a theocentric view. It must be a practice, a normal approach.

If Temptation Knocks, Yield?

Take Genesis 39. Not as difficult as Genesis 37 nor as scary as Genesis 38, and Mrs. Potiphar certainly makes it interesting. Indeed she may tempt *us* as much as she did Joseph. It wouldn't be hard to gravitate to verses 7-12 and begin to develop 'Principles for resisting temptation.' I can draw out at least four of them from this section of the text. You may be able to do 'better' than that.

But what if we keep our eyes off of Potiphar's wife and keep them on the living God – or simply *read* the text carefully? Then we notice, don't we, that the writer wraps his story with a distinct theological emphasis – 'Yahweh was with Joseph' (vv. 2, 3, 21, 23)? The fact that this keynote occurs twice at the beginning and twice at the end of the narrative may mean that we are to regard everything in the whole story as depicting Yahweh's presence with his servant. Is Genesis 39 then not indicating the various circumstances in which Joseph enjoyed Yahweh's presence? Hence, Yahweh is with his servant (1) in his forsakenness, verses 1-6; (2) in his temptation, verses 7-18; and (3) in his disillusionment, verses 19-23.[3] Isn't this more in line with the expressed theological emphasis of the writer? Doesn't it yield richer applicatory possibilities than the 'resisting temptation' focus? I am not saying we should not analyze Joseph's encounter with Potiphar's wife and derive practical help from it (after all, note the theology of v. 9). But to the degree that we concentrate only on that we miss the premier point the writer is making about Yahweh's presence; and we may neglect his implicit argument that the reason Joseph resisted temptation was not so much because he followed four (or however many) principles but because Yahweh was 'with him.' Can you see how we can strip God of his glory by our inadequate interpretation? Joseph, thankfully, escaped the clutches of Potiphar's wife but maybe far too many interpreters have been seduced into hermeneutical bed with her.

Riddled with theology

Please look at 1 Samuel 16:1-13. If we were merely analyzing the story we might list the components as:

> Samuel comes to Bethlehem, vv. 1-5
> Samuel's wrong move, vv. 6-7
> An embarrassing moment, vv. 8-11
> David arrives, vv. 12-13

But that won't preach – nor should it. It's not telling us what Yahweh is doing. Of course, we might note verse 7 and realize that it is a significant theological note – and we'd be right. But the whole passage needs viewed 'God-wardly.' If we do that, we will no longer look at it as several scenes revolving around human characters but as a revelation of God, to which even the heifer makes her contribution. So I prefer treating the passage something like this:

> I. The God who provides for his kingdom, v. 1
> II. The God who stoops to our fears, vv. 2-5a
> III. The God who prevents our folly, vv. 5b-7
> IV. The God who reverses our conventions, vv. 8-13

Will this preach? I think so. In point I., I would pick up on Samuel's mourning over Saul. Apparently Samuel held that king in some affection; at least he was likely distressed over what disaster might overtake Israel now that Yahweh had publicly rejected Saul. But Yahweh has work for Samuel – to go to Jesse's place in Bethlehem, 'for I have seen among his sons a king for myself' (v. 1). Yahweh is telling Samuel that though it may look like the kingdom is going down the tube, he knows the next step and has provided what his kingdom needs in order to go on. How easily in any historical moment we can fear the people of God are about to go under and the Lord must assure us, 'Now, look, I am not caught unprepared – I am ready to supply what my people need in this dark hour.' Jesus knew all about the 'gates of Hades' but didn't think they could keep him from building his church (Matt. 16:18).

But of course the 'next step' is a problem for Samuel. Saul has his agents out – if Samuel goes to Bethlehem Saul will have his head (v. 2a). Then we see that the Lord not only provides kings but heifers as well (v. 2b). Samuel can go to Bethlehem under the 'cover' of convening a sacrificial feast and no one will be the wiser.[4] And so he does. But don't you see what point II. tells you about God? These little, scrawny verses, this mere conversation between God and his prophet? See how God takes notice of and addresses Samuel's fears? He does not mock or ridicule him or tell him he'd never make a decent rugby player. He doesn't jeer at him for trembling before Saul's sword (cf. Ps. 103:14). Is he not the same God with us? Does he not understand what terrifies us? Perhaps the fear that we'll not be saved at the last because we have no assurance of salvation now? Or are you alone in the world and wonder who is going to care for you when darker days come? Though you are one of Christ's flock, do you have a terror of dying? Have you a spouse who is abandoning you and you can't imagine how you will get on? Do you see Samuel's God? He does not despise you in your fears but stoops down to meet you in them.

Point III. begins by underscoring the peril of our impressions. Yahweh had 'seen' (lit., v. 1) a king among Jesse's sons and Samuel thought he saw him right off. Something about Eliab – maybe his build, the way he carried himself among people, or his aftershave. Who knows? But he knew Eliab had 'king' written all over him (v. 6). And so Yahweh had to assert the principle of his operation – that he is the One who can and does inspect men's hearts, and so Eliab was a reject (v. 7). Eliab outwardly must have been as impressive as Saul (1 Sam. 9:1-2; 10:23-24). And that was the problem. Had Samuel had his way he would have anointed another 'Saul,' and Israel would have been heading for another disaster.

Yahweh, however, kept Samuel from falling for the deceptiveness of the obvious. Something like that Associated Press story of Linda Burnett, who went for groceries at her neighborhood supermarket. She was seen sitting in her car, doors locked and windows rolled up, eyes closed, hands behind her head. A man asked if she was all right; she said she'd been shot in the back of the head and had been holding her brains in for over an hour. Paramedics were summoned. They broke into the car and found Linda had a wad of bread dough on the back of her head. A Pillsbury biscuit canister had exploded from the heat, sounded like a gunshot, and the dough smacked her in the back of the head. The stuff she felt was bread not brains, and shampoo not surgery was the fix. But it *seemed* convincing. What would you do if you heard a shot and then got whacked in the back of your head?

And Eliab *seemed* every inch a king. And Samuel fell for it. All of which tells us that not even the finest and godliest leaders can be trusted with God's kingdom without God's wisdom. But Yahweh, who looks on the heart, kept Samuel from being trigger-happy with his horn of oil. Is this not frequently his way with his servants? Can't you itemize any number of times God has *kept you from* stupid, disastrous choices? Shouldn't we love this God for the saving obstacles he puts in place?

Then it gets rather embarrassing at the church supper, because Samuel has to tell Jesse repeatedly, 'Yahweh has not chosen this one.' When they run out of candidates, Samuel asks Jesse the obvious question and finds out he has a youngest son who was not thought to be 'in the running' and so was left to work the sheep. He is called, brought, and anointed, and once more Scripture teaches us that the Lord chooses the most unlikely folk to do his will and accomplish his purposes and that he frequently stands human standards and human expectations on their boring heads – and so remains the interesting and refreshing God he is.

Isn't 1 Samuel 16:1-13 a bonnie word for the church in any age, especially when she cannot see what is ahead for her in times of crisis (which is most of the time)? The text says to her, 'You will be all right as long as you have this God – this God who is adequate and kind and wise and different.' It's all about him. And it is this constant theocentric perspective that must grab hold of us if we are to make right use of Old Testament narrative.

An Adventurous Courage

I look on that 'constant perspective' as the primary prerequisite in keeping us 'on center' in our biblical interpretation. However, there are lesser prerequisites that may prove vital at any time. One of these I would dub 'an adventurous courage.'

Let me explain what I mean by this phrase. If our interpretive approach is God-focused, then we will often find ourselves bumping into the sovereignty of God in our texts. That should be no problem but we may think it is. It may bring up 'difficulties' – like how it meshes with human responsibility. Some of our hearers may have problems along these lines and so we may think it better to keep on themes about coping in the Christian life, rather than stirring their minds with theological conundrums. The text may be clear, but we don't want to go there. And I am simply saying, 'No, you should.' In the difficulties are the treasures. In short, we must go wherever the teaching of the text leads us, even if

it's into the mysteries of God. What other mysteries matter
so much? No, we don't want to get into theological debates
merely to fuel debate.[5] But we are studying the wrong book if
we hope to avoid theology!

So there will be theology and doctrine and maybe, for
some, very disturbing doctrine. Well, welcome to the Bible!
For the Bible is a very doctrinal book – in fact, I find that
most of my preaching is little else than a filling out of the
doctrine of God, expounding the wonder and ways of the
Trinity. But where better to preach this disturbing doctrine
than in narrative texts, where folks can see (if they are awake)
the doctrinal bones clothed in narrative flesh?

Take a sample: 2 Samuel 17. David is on the run, has
abandoned Jerusalem, and Absalom is plotting how best to
follow up his successful coup. Ahithophel, David's former
premier counselor-turned-traitor, advises Absalom how to
exterminate David and win the people's loyalty for himself
(vv. 1-4). Absalom & Co. are quite impressed with this
advice – it seems vintage Ahithophel (cf. 16:23). For some
reason Absalom also asks Hushai, David's friend who had
seemingly turned pro-Absalom (16:16-19), what they should
do. Absalom tells Hushai what Ahithophel's advice was (v. 6).
Hushai does the unthinkable; he begins by telling them that
'this time' Ahithophel has really missed the train. Hushai
launches into a wordy, picturesque, flattering bit of rhetoric
(vv. 8-13) that carries the day with Absalom and his cronies
(v. 14a). Then we read the secret behind it all:

> Now *Yahweh* [emphatic] had ordained to frustrate
> Ahithophel's 'good' counsel, in order that Yahweh might
> bring disaster upon Absalom (v. 14b).

As you survey 2 Samuel 17:1-24, you must admit that
verse 14b is the theological boulder placed in the middle
of the story and meant to serve as the anchor of the whole
account. It's almost a flashing neon text. Admittedly, there
is something nasty about it, because it teaches that Yahweh

wants to bring disaster on Absalom and decided he would
do so by overturning what would have been Ahithophel's
successful advice. But then Yahweh's judgment is never cozy
or comfy.

Now, of course, you could spend your time here, as one
expositor has done, talking about 'the hazard of self-interest,'
about how Absalom lacked the fortitude to press on in his evil
plan, and about how irresolution often plagues those given to
self-interest, and then give but a passing acknowledgement
of verse 14b (I withhold documentation to protect the dead).
But verse 14b places the stress on Yahweh's sovereignty rather
than Absalom's psychology. How might we preach the text if
we allowed the writer's obvious intention to guide us?

We cannot develop the passage completely, but I would
propose it highlights two emphases about Yahweh's
sovereignty. First, *the secret of his sovereignty*. What strikes
us about the way God's 'ordination' works out is that it seems
so natural, so unobtrusive. After Ahithophel's counsel is
given in verses 1-4, we may fear it's curtain time for David.
But then Hushai gives his advice, souped up as it is with
flourishes of language and vivid description: he appeals to
Absalom's *knowledge* (v. 8 – 'you' is emphatic, i.e., Absalom
is aware of this, though Ahithophel may have temporary
amnesia), *caution/fear* (vv. 9-10, as if to say, 'There's a fine
line, Absalom, between impetuosity and stupidity'), *pride*
(v. 11), and *hatred* (vv. 12-13). Ahithophel knew how to get
things done successfully; Hushai knew what moves men
with evil hearts. But then you read the secret, verse 14b, and
that keeps you from singing the doxology to Hushai – he was
simply the shrewd instrument of Yahweh's will to put an
end to Absalom. But it's all so natural, so hidden. And that
is supremely comforting, for it tells us that no matter how
successful evil men and evil purposes seem to be they are not
outside the firm grip of Yahweh's control. And the fact that
his sovereignty works so secretly and hiddenly simply adds
to its interest and mystique.

Second, the passage points to *the victory of his sovereignty*. All the certainty of verse 14b gives way to apparent uncertainty in what follows. They dismiss Hushai from the strategy session without telling him they are going to follow his counsel. All Hushai can do is try to get updated news of the state of affairs to David. That proves to be a harum-scarum adventure in itself (vv. 15-22). But all works for the protection of David. Ahithophel seems to divine the coming disaster for Absalom: David will now have time to re-coup and his men will knock the tar out of Absalom's forces. Ahithophel apparently considered a quiet, domestic suicide preferable to a public execution for treason by a restored David (v. 23). Yet Ahithophel's end is more than simply a private suicide. It highlights the shameful and sure end decreed for those who dare to assault Yahweh's chosen king and kingdom. There is a 'larger point' here, a 'last things' implication: the overthrow of this royal betrayer is a picture of what will happen to all who seek to overturn the kingdom of the true and greater David, the Lord Jesus Christ. They do so at their own peril, for Yahweh is watching over his King and his kingdom to protect them from falling. 'His kingdom cannot fail!'

It's tragic then if you get the 'willies' because verse 14 is so theological and sovereignty-driven, for then your people will not hear how fascinating Yahweh's ways are nor how secure his kingdom is; they will miss out on both interesting instruction and solid encouragement. The Holy Spirit intends verse 14b as a magnet to suck you right to the core truth of the narrative. It's doctrinal. Could be controversial. If you're paranoid about it, get over it.

A certain viciousness

If God's character, ways, and work are to be the focus of our interpretation, then we must deal nastily with temptations to become absorbed in secondary matters. Some of us are possessed with such a compulsion for thoroughness (normally a virtue) that we want to solve all the difficulties or conundrums in our text – and lead our people through them – before we ever get to the teaching of the text; all of which can dull, dim, and deaden the teaching.

So if we preach on 2 Kings 5 we may feel compelled to tackle Naaman's leprosy, whether it was Hansen's disease or what precisely it might have been. We might delineate what Leviticus teaches about leprosy in Israel and what we don't know about leprosy in Syria, taking the first five minutes of our sermon to treat a disease.

This is understandable. As we study a text, we feel we have to understand that text and its background and, if there are particular difficulties in the text, we want to have a handle on them and be able to know where we stand on them. But we must remember that there's a huge amount of stuff that we study that we *don't* bring into the pulpit. Now I know that we need to be thinking what questions our people might have about a text, ones that may perplex them, and we don't want to be thoughtless on that score. And, of course, if you don't give full coverage to, say, Naaman's leprosy, you're sure to have some character come up to you afterwards who has always had a special interest in biblical 'leprosy' and biblical diseases and who has read a 1982 article by a gynecologist in Tasmania whose hobby is ancient dermatology and who proposes a hitherto unproposed proposal about, of all people, Naaman's disease.

But there are some people who need to be ignored. Once in Reformed Seminary chapel, then professor of homiletics Dr. Roy Taylor told us that his sermon on his selected text was going to be a 'freeway' sermon. He meant that he was going to keep to the main highway, speeding on to, and with, the main thrust of his text, and not 'getting off' at every interesting 'exit' along the way. That is often a good model for our work. Having a theocentric preoccupation will slough off scads of unnecessary distractions.

Joshua 2 is a useful case in point. Here lies the problem of Rahab's lie to the Jericho police. Of course we can take the time to go into the ethical problem and talk about 'what if Nazis came to your door' asking if you were concealing Jews. Let me stop and say what I am not saying. I am not recommending we ignore such difficulties in our texts. There are likely some cultures in which the expositor would have to deal rather thoroughly with the dilemma of 'Rahab's lie.' I am only begging that we not become so 'hung up' on such problems that we never hear the testimony the text wants to give.

In Joshua 2 the structure boxes off the testimony. Note the lay-out:[6]

> Commission by Joshua, v. 1a
>   Arrival/concern: Protection of the spies, vv. 1b-7
>   Confession of faith, vv. 8-14
>   Escape/concern: Protection of Rahab & Co., vv. 15-21
> Return to Joshua, vv. 22-24

Notice the cliffhanger at the end of verse 7. The reader has a mild anxiety attack. You wonder: How will those two fellows get out if the city gates have been shut? And note that the writer doesn't bring you relief until verses 15ff. In between, in verses 8-14, in the very center of the story, he places Rahab's confession of faith. It's a marvelous summary, by the way, for teaching the components of genuine faith:

> Communication: Hearing the might of Yahweh, v. 10
> Conviction: Confessing the majesty of Yahweh, v. 11
> Commitment: Fleeing to the mercy of Yahweh, vv. 12-13

Faith moves from testimony to persuasion to venturing. All this is the center and focus of the writer's story. This is *Rahab's truth*. But what can easily be our tendency in Joshua 2? Oh, here is an ethical problem. How will I explain this? How many 'views' are there about it? Though to a certain extent we need to acknowledge such items, we tend to be consumed by them and fasten on them and take our eyes off what the writer has conspired to tell us. Imagine how the writer of Joshua must feel when he hears our 'Rahab' sermons: 'That guy did it too! What more can I do? I place Rahab's confession of Yahweh's supremacy smack-dab in the middle of this text, and does he see it? Does he hear it? I show by cutting things off at verse 7 that what happens to the spies doesn't really matter; I so much as say, "Get a load of this!" right before verse 8; and here is the preacher worrying about why a pagan, Canaanite call-girl didn't have higher moral standards! Ugh – what more can I do?' In this text we must not let Rahab's lie eclipse Rahab's truth. And in general I am only saying we need to go for the gold rather than piddle with the difficulties when preaching.

You will face this temptation to dwell on lesser things in any number of narrative texts. You are in 1 Kings 20 and you run into the story of the prophet who will confront Ahab. There's that strange clip that tells how this prophet told a fellow to strike him and the fellow refused; so the prophet told the man he'd be killed by a lion – and he was (vv. 35-36). Now you can moan about how you can't preach that text, or you can try to discern what the text is saying about the word of Yahweh that comes through his prophet. Or in 1 Kings 22 you can happen on to Micaiah's telling about his vision about how Yahweh was going to entice and lure Ahab to his own destruction (vv. 19-23); one could get nervous over how devious Yahweh seems to be. But of course it's a non-existent problem. What's devious about telling Ahab that you intend to be devious? Or you go to Judges 3 and look on Eglon's massive bulk lying in his special latrine. But if you get past the guts and the gore and see Judges 3:12-30 as it intends, a story of how Yahweh saves his people, it will do wonders for your eschatology, for it will assure you that there will be a lot more fat slobs dumped into the landfill of history as Yahweh goes on defending his people. But we must be vicious with ourselves or we'll always be traveling hermeneutical side roads.

A driving passion

There was a lady in the early 1700s who was present at an observance of the Lord's supper where Ebenezer Erskine was assisting. She was very moved by Erskine's exposition. She found out who he was and next Lord's Day was in Erskine's own place of worship to hear him. But it fell flat; she simply wasn't stirred as she had been at the previous communion service. Perplexed about this, she called on Erskine to inquire about it. (If a preacher fails to move you, who better to ask about it than the preacher himself?) Why was there such a difference in her feelings? Erskine replied, 'Madam, the reason is this – last Sabbath you went to hear Jesus Christ; but today, you have come to hear Ebenezer Erskine.'[7]

I wonder if our problems in biblical interpretation might be a bit like that. Some will likely accuse me of being 'over the top' here. Still, I wonder if a good chunk of our hermeneutical problem may simply be a heart problem. Maybe we get off the track in our interpretation because our eyes are fastened on the wrong object.

I often feel like the spiritual pigmy I am when I read the words of the sons of Korah in Psalm 43:3-4:

> Oh send out thy light and thy truth;
> let them lead me,
> let them bring me to thy holy hill and to thy dwelling!
> Then I will go to the altar of God,
> to God my exceeding joy... (RSV)

God – my exceeding joy. Do I usually think of him that way? Seek him as such? Have this God as the center of my vision? Must he, should he not be such even in – especially in – my biblical interpretation? Maybe our problem is a spiritual one. Maybe we are not salivating for the triune God as we read our Bibles. Maybe we are seeking sermons and not him. Maybe we are looking for Bible studies rather than for the Holy One of Israel. Maybe it's a matter of worship.

Addendum (can be skipped)

This chapter will prove a disappointment to some who would hold that our Old Testament exposition should be not merely *theocentric* but clearly *Christocentric*. I have no desire for controversy, but I probably ought to defend myself a bit for taking what I judge to be a minority view among evangelical interpreters.

The question is not: Should we preach Christ from Old Testament texts? (Answer: Yes); but: *Must* we preach Christ from *every* Old Testament text? Quite a number would say so. Why? Some would say, Because Jesus says so. They point to his statements in John 5:39-40, 46, and in Luke 24:25-27, 44-47, and, on this basis hold that Jesus affirms that every text in the Bible speaks of himself.

Because Luke 24 is pivotal we should note what it tells us about Jesus and the Old Testament: (1) Jesus is concerned with the *totality* of the Old Testament's witness (v. 25, 'all that the prophets have spoken'; v. 44, it was necessary for '*all things* written in the law of Moses and in the prophets and in the psalms...'), particularly its witness of the *sufferings* of the Messiah prior to his glory (vv. 26, 46); (2) there is a wide *scope* of Old Testament materials in which this testimony to Christ can be found (note: v. 27a, from Moses and from all the prophets; v. 44b, things written in the law of Moses and the prophets and the psalms; this in the face of the claims of anti-supernaturalist biblical criticism); witness to the Messiah is found in all parts of the Old Testament; (3) the witness of the Old Testament scriptures carries a particular *focus* upon the Messiah himself (v. 27b, 'the things concerning himself'; v. 44, 'all the things written...concerning me'). These may overlap somewhat, but this summarizes, I think, Jesus' claims in Luke 24.

From Jesus' statements I make an inference and form a corollary: the whole Old Testament bears witness to Christ; and, the Old Testament does not bear witness only to Christ. Why this corollary? Because I agree with making an *extensive* inference from Luke 24:27 and 44 but hold that an *intensive* inference is illegitimate. What on earth does that mean? It means I think Jesus is teaching that *all parts* of the Old Testament testify of the Messiah in his suffering and glory, but I do not think Jesus is saying that *every* Old Testament passage/text bears witness to him. Jesus referred to the things written about him *in* the law of Moses, the prophets, and the psalms – he did not say that every passage spoke of him (v. 44). Therefore, I do not feel compelled to make every Old Testament (narrative) passage point to Christ in some way because I do not think Christ himself requires it.

Not every Old Testament exposition then must end up speaking directly of Christ, because (1) Jesus does not demand it, and, in addition, (2) such a regimen impoverishes Old Testament exposition. How would the latter happen? Well, if Old Testament exposition must in some way speak of Christ and if the textual theology of an Old Testament passage does not (seem to) do so, will that not be eliminated as unworthy exposition?

Some examples. First Samuel 25 tells how Yahweh (through Abigail) restrained his servant David from his own impulsive and bloody design on Nabal and his household. The restraint theme pervades the text (vv. 26, 33, 34, 39). Does the text not show how Yahweh graciously and firmly intercepts his servants on the road to folly (though not always via a lovely female)? Does he only do that for his chosen king or for us as well? If so, should I not point out to the Lord's people how the Lord's hands often lovingly construct roadblocks to our determined foolishness? Must I somehow run this point through a Christological sieve before it can become legitimate exposition or application?

Or take 1 Samuel 4:3. It's loaded with theology. Bad theology. It's the bright idea of Israel's elders to get the ark of the covenant and 'let it come among us and save us from the hand of our enemies.' A case of covenant people with pagan minds. Israel seems to think that if they have God's furniture they must have God's power; should anything happen to the ark it would wreck Yahweh's reputation (he would appear to be the 'defeated' god) and he wouldn't *dare* let that happen. So they have God right where they want him – in their hands. Another case of attempted deity-hijacking. And don't we find parallels to this bad theology among God's professing people today? Don't we have our 'evangelical' tactics for putting God under pressure? Though we may practice it with more sophistication are we not often adherents of rabbit-foot religion? This particular exposition and application, however, can be developed without explicit reference to Christ. Does that invalidate this point as Christian proclamation?

Or go to 1 Kings 17:17-24. Were I preaching this passage I would want to lead from Yahweh's defeat of death in verses 23-24 to Christ's triumph over it in, say, Mark 5:21-43, Luke 7:11-17, and John 11, and then fully in his resurrection (cf. 2 Tim. 1:10!). But what about verses 17-18? Doesn't it strike us that here is a woman in desperate need (vv. 10-12), who embraces a divine promise (vv. 13-14) and enjoys a steady provision (vv. 15-16) – only to be crushed with death and sorrow (vv. 17-18)? The God who promises to sustain life now takes life away. Isn't there some of Gilead's balm seeping from this text for some of the Lord's contemporary people? Aren't there believers (some of them recent ones, like this widow) in our assemblies who know exactly what this widow faced? They enjoy the Lord's smile upon their tent and then he seems to plunge them into the pit. It is simply a part of believing experience, and when we see it set out clearly in an Old Testament narrative, the text cries out for us to set it before God's people. Simply to see this sequence from enjoyment to despair, from God's provision to his severity, amazingly comforts saints. They sense that God's word (and therefore God) understands them and strangely they have fresh hope. But there is nothing overtly Christological about this point; this does not directly 'preach Christ.' So am I to assume that this point should not be pressed upon my hearers, that the God of all comfort will have to find another vehicle for his consoling work?[8]

I have no problem in preaching Christ from an Old Testament narrative so long as this can be done legitimately – and it frequently can. Look back at 1 Samuel 16:1-13. If one presses home the surprise of God's choice in verses 8-12 of that text, can one not go on to point out that the same was true of David's Descendant? Folks could say there were all sorts of reasons why Jesus could not be God's chosen king: He's just one of us (Mark 6:2-3); he has too much fun (Matt. 11:18-19); he's not from the right place (John 7:41-42); Messiahs don't suffer (Matt. 27:42-43). But the One who is rejected by men is chosen and precious in the sight of God (1 Peter 2:4) – *and* in the sight of his people (1 Peter 2:7).

Can one not also rightly point to Christ simply from the *pattern* of David's experience that begins in 1 Samuel 16:13, when the Spirit of Yahweh rushed upon him to equip him for his task? No sooner does the Spirit rush upon David than he is catapulted into chapter-upon-chapter of trouble – the envy, anger, and plots of Saul, all the way to the end of 1 Samuel. David, the man with Yahweh's Spirit will be hunted and betrayed, trapped and escaping, hiding in caves, running from death, living in exile, driven to the edge. The Spirit comes, the trouble begins. Was it not the same with David's son and David's Lord? What could be more heartening than the Spirit's descent and the Father's voice at his baptism (Mark 1:11)? Then the wilderness, the temptation, the enemy (1:12-13). And all the rest. And the same pattern for his people (Acts 14:22).

So I am not against preaching Christ from Old Testament narrative texts. If one argues from biblical texts that there are certain biblical grounds for divorce, that doesn't mean one is pro-divorce. And just because I don't think every Old Testament text is about Christ does not mean I oppose preaching Christ from Old Testament texts if he is legitimately to be seen there. Someone might ask why my own Old

Testament exposition doesn't have more of a Christological bent than it does. The answer is simple: I am not as skilled at it as a good number of others are. However, I am convinced that I do not honor Christ by forcing him into texts where he is not.

Endnotes

1. Walker Percy, *The Second Coming* (New York: Farrar, Straus, Giroux, 1980), 152.

2. You can see this sketched out for all of Old Testament teaching in the outline and development of Paul R. House's *Old Testament Theology* (Downers Grove: InterVarsity, 1998).

3. I may be overdoing it in the last item. I am only trying to capture how Joseph might well have looked on his prison stint at the first: he does what is right, resists temptation, honors his master, gets framed, and – for all his fidelity – ends up in the slammer.

4. There was nothing unethical in this. Samuel was not under obligation to inform Saul of his total agenda. For discussion, see John Murray, *Principles of Conduct* (Grand Rapids: Eerdmans, 1957), 139-41.

5. There are some who simply make trouble for themselves in the way they preach or teach God's sovereignty; that is, some have such an in-your-face attitude that it is no wonder their people are turned off or resistant. I am convinced that there is often a sneaky yet ethical way to preach these themes simply from biblical texts (like narratives!) without using the loaded buzz-words that sometimes set folks off. Nevertheless, some will choose to be offended anyway, which means that either they – or I! – may need to find another church. All the same, we must not allow a phobia over doctrinal controversy to keep us from God-centered proclamation.

6. Taken with slight change from my *Joshua: No Falling Words* (Ross-shire: Christian Focus, 2000), 25.

7. John Whitecross, *The Shorter Catechism Illustrated from Christian Biography and History* (reprint ed., London: Banner of Truth, 1968), 144.

8. I think that expositors can also be so focused on Christological connections that they simply miss some of this more mundane theology in the text. I can think of a sermon summary I saw on Genesis 22; the expositor seemed so concerned to draw out the links to Christ that he ignored the huge theological problem (viz., that God seemed to contradict his own promise and plan) right at the first of the narrative.

CHAPTER 9

Synthesis

We have been looking at various 'pieces' that go into preaching Old Testament narratives. I think it might be useful to conclude with a little exercise in bringing it all together. How might all the 'pieces' flow together into a coherent exposition? We may take Exodus 1–2 as our sample section. I want to work briefly through each section of the text making *observations* and then indicate how these observations feed into *exposition*. With Exodus 2, I will make section-by-section observations, with some interim comments, but will hold off the sample exposition and treat the chapter as a whole. If readers follow the various headings I don't think confusion will reign.

Observations on Exodus 1:1-22

Hardly the finest marketing technique – opening a book with all these names (vv. 1-5)! Makes perfect sense, however, if one realizes that in one sense the chapter is all about people.

That raises the premier question: what is the chapter about? So one carefully slides over the text hoping to find out. Sometimes, repetition will furnish a clue – and does here. For one notices a low-key sort of repetition, not exact but obvious enough, in verses 7, 12, and 20:

> But the sons of Israel were fruitful, and there were swarms of them, and they multiplied and became very, very strong – and the land was filled with them (v. 7).

> But the more they afflicted them, the more they multiplied and burst out (v. 12a).
>
> So the people multiplied and became very strong (v. 20b).

Have we a writer who is simply fascinated with the birth-rates of minorities? Why this repetition? Hopefully we are coming at Exodus 1 fresh from Genesis 12–50 and recognize that verses 7, 12, and 20 highlight the fulfillment of the people-promise in Genesis 12:2, 15:5, 17:6, 22:17, 26:4, and 28:14, Yahweh's assurance to Abraham, Isaac, and Jacob. Here is that promise coming to pass in less than ideal conditions. The chapter is about God's faithfulness to his promises, or simply, about the Promise-keeper.

All this is helpful because it tells us what the chapter is *not* about. It is not about the new king who did not know/ acknowledge Joseph (v. 8) – much as we'd like to nail down his identity and solve our chronological problems. It's not about the exact location of the storage cities (v. 11) or the ethics of the midwives (v. 19).[1] We should try to know what we can about historical, geographical, archaeological, and ethical matters related to the text, but must not allow all that to take our fingers off the theological jugular vein we've discovered.

There are a few more observations to make. For example, does the turn of affairs in verses 8-14 surprise us as Bible readers?[2] Not if we remember the Lord's clear word to Abraham in Genesis 15:13-14.[3] All of which uncovers an interesting twist: 'But what impresses us in the light of Genesis 15:13 is that in the oppression Pharaoh and his people carried out God's will without being aware of it.'[4] Had he known – that would have put the fire in Pharaoh's ire!

Briefly: (1) Note we are given the midwives' personal names (v. 15); no such dignity is accorded the king of Egypt – he simply goes by the generic 'Pharaoh';[5] (2) the chapter closes (v. 22) on a note of suspense; the story does continue in chapter 2 but that is a distinct segment of it; verse 22 leaves readers hanging with the latest crisis in front of them; and (3) note that there is sparse reference to God in chapter 1; he never talks; Pharaoh does most all the talking (vv. 9, 15, 18, 22).

Exposition of Exodus 1

How might one pull Exodus 1 together in an expository approach? I would begin with those names (vv. 1-5) and explain that the reason we meet all these names is because God's people matter to him. And, on the basis of my study of the chapter, I would announce that the chapter is trying to teach that *God is careful to keep his promises to the people who matter to him.* So the general theme is the faithfulness of God, and I would begin by underscoring *the silence of God's faithfulness.* Here I want to help hearers discover verses 7, 12, and 20, so they see what the chapter is about. They may have to get their promise-goggles on to see these verses and how they link with the people-promise in Genesis.[6] Then I want hearers to see the manner of God's faithfulness, i.e., to *hear* the *silence* of it. I want to tell them there is no fanfare in this text, no place where we read anything like, 'Then Yahweh said, "Behold I am about to fulfill the promise I made..."' None of that. God never talks (is only mentioned three times near the end of the chapter); Pharaoh does all the talking. All we know about what God is about are these three little subversive sentences in verses 7, 12, and 20. Application can find several directions; one might be that we may fail to see God's faithfulness in our own circumstances because we only expect it in spectacular or dramatic forms.

I would want to stress, from verses 8-14, *the secret of God's faithfulness.* Not only Israel's growth but even their affliction reveals his faithfulness, because their affliction is the fulfillment of his word in Genesis 15:13. And there is the additional ironic twist (a la Gispen) that in oppressing Israel Pharaoh & Co. are carrying out Yahweh's word without being aware of it. You find the same stuff in the church's prayer in Acts 4:27-28. If the power-brokers of this age knew they were nothing but God's lackeys, it'd knock the strut out of their step. Even in general here we are left with a paradox: Israel's affliction is the fulfillment of God's word and therefore evidence of his faithfulness. Don't we face the same mystery? Isn't our Lord's word that 'through many tribulations we must enter the kingdom of God' (Acts 14:22)? My adversities then are not evidence of God's betrayal or neglect but of his consistency.

In the gutsy midwives (vv. 15-21) we see *the servants of God's faithfulness*. They may have been the leaders of midwives' Local 311. In any case, they did not cooperate. God is faithful and uses the midwives to maintain his faithfulness (note v. 20b). 'What is remarkable is that the names of these lowly women are recorded whereas, by contrast, the all-powerful reigning monarch is consistently veiled in anonymity. In this way the biblical narrator expresses his scale of values.'[7] Two women frustrate the tyrant's decree – at least momentarily. The midwives teach us that we should never be too surprised at the vast array of instruments God uses in showing his faithfulness to us – they will frequently be ones we never dreamed of.[8]

Finally, the text leaves us with *the suspense of God's faithfulness* (v. 22). Enough of politicking with midwives. Pharaoh's new policy puts every Egyptian citizen under obligation to engage in genocide. This is the fresh emergency and the end of the chapter. We are left on the edge of a literary cliff. Now what?

A little thought tells us what the writer wants us to do. Wouldn't he want us to look at God's previous record? What had happened in the face of passing time (vv. 1-6)? God's promise goes on (v. 7). What about heavy affliction (vv. 8-11, 13-14)? God's promise proves tougher (v. 12). But what if there is blatant tyranny (vv. 15-16, 18)? Still the promise rather than Pharaoh rules (v. 20b). The writer wants you to use a bit of logic: if God has proven faithful previously in the face of time (vv. 1-7), trouble (vv. 8-14), and tyranny

(vv. 15-21), then can't his people trust him in face of every new crisis (v. 22)? The point is: The God who has held you all through Exodus 1 will not let go of you after verse 22.

A number of years ago *Time* magazine ran a feature article entitled, 'Sex and Suffering in the Afternoon.' It was about TV soap operas. (I don't watch them – I simply read the article). It said that a soap's writers tried to script some sort of unresolved crisis for the Friday afternoon episode. This was considered essential as a 'hook' to make viewers return to the show after the week-end break. With the soaps suspense is a gimmick, in life it is too frequently a fact. And we wonder – how will we meet this one? How can we get through this new loss or this fresh trouble? Answer: by resting in the same God who has held us and carried us through every other one.

Observations on Exodus 2:1-10

How generic this passage is! No one has a name – well, not until 'Moses' hits print in verse 10. Until then he's simply the 'child' (seven times). His father is a 'man from the house of Levi' (v. 1), his mother a 'daughter of Levi' (v. 1) or 'the woman' (v. 2) or the 'mother of the child' (v. 8); filling out the female cast are 'his sister' (v. 4) and the 'daughter of Pharaoh' (v. 5), plus a few of her attendants. But no names. And while we're at it, God is conspicuous by his absence – there is no mention of God. He is not there.

We feel a twinge of anguish as we read the word 'son' in verse 2, because we've just read what Pharaoh has ordered for such male babies in 1:22. A ray of hope joins our anguish, however, when we read about his miniscule 'ark' (vv. 3, 5) the mother weaves and waterproofs; we feel hope, for the only other place we find this word (*tēbâ*) is in Genesis 6–9; granted, a much larger edition but a vehicle of deliverance in danger nevertheless.

I will not discuss the way the writer ratchets up the tension and suspense at verses 5-6. Allow me to refer you to my comments on that near the end of chapter 2. However, we must notice the humor in the episode (vv. 6ff.): (1) Pharaoh's own daughter frustrates Pharaoh's decree – at least in this signal case;[9] (2) his own mother gets to be the child's nurse; (3) his mother gets a regular government cheque for providing Kiddie Kare for her own kid; and (4) the child is raised under state protection. Heaven is laughing.

Interim Comments on Exodus 2:1-10

For our expository sample I prefer to treat all of Exodus 2 together. However, 2:1-10 can rightly be preached by itself and, should one do so, I simply want to offer a couple of comments on that.

Here is an account of God's delightful providence. When we preach this text, however, we know that any number of the Lord's flock may know more of his hard than of his happy providences at present. I think it may help (perhaps in one's conclusion) to recognize that Exodus 1:1-2:10 suggests that not all Israelite parents had a 'Moses story' to tell. Moses' mother had one. But how many Israelite parents must've had Pharaoh's police pay them a call, rip their infant lad out of their desperate clutches – then they watched in helpless rage and furious grief as the little tyke was flipped into the Nile, because 'it's the law, you know'? Moses' parents enjoyed God's marvelous providence but many more knew his mysterious providence – and it's important to remember we meet both in the course of Christian experience. The situation is precisely the same in Matthew 2:13-23, where Jesus enjoys a 'Moses experience,' where Egypt proved, ironically, a haven of safety for him. But not so for most toddlers in greater Bethlehem. Herod's thugs paid house visits and butchered them all (2:16). I think it is well to keep such matters in mind. The emphasis of the text should excite us over the wonders of God's providence, and yet the aches of God's people should keep us from ignoring the perplexity of it. Then we see the real promise of the text: providence doesn't always keep the church from her fears but only from her extinction. More on this in a bit.

I think we must also clearly understand the goal of 2:1-10, what this text is wanting you to do in response to what it tells you. This can be a tricky matter. As we read of baby Moses' preservation we (I should think) consider it an episode of what we call theologically God's providence. And it is here we may miss the boat. For the goal of the text is not to get you to say, 'My, isn't providence a bonnie doctrine?' Rather, the text is calling you: 'Come, let us adore him!' Doctrinal appreciation may feed genuine worship but it should never be identified with it. In our finest hermeneutical moments we are only a step from idolatry.

Observations on Exodus 2:11-22

In verse 10 Moses is an infant; in verse 11 he is grown and, apparently, off on his life's work. What a time gap between verses 10 and 11! This is no continuous biography of Moses. And immediately we run into a bloody business (vv. 11b-12):

> And he saw an Egyptian man striking a Hebrew man, one of his brothers. So he turned this way and that and he saw that there was no one there; so he struck down the Egyptian and hid him in the sand.

One way or another an expositor has to deal with this episode. The usual tack is to say that Moses is a murderer and that he likely moved ahead without a divine call to do so. But I'm not convinced; I'm not sure Moses did wrong; he may have committed justice rather than murder.[10] Note, by the way, that Moses involves himself in three episodes in the text in which he seeks to right wrongs and bring deliverance – a foregleam of his future work. But what, after all, do you do when an Egyptian is beating the daylights out of a Hebrew? Turn your back and quote Romans 13? Do you comfort yourself with the thought that the beating may not prove fatal (perhaps the victim will only be maimed?) and so best not to intervene? Moses (blessed man) did not have a cell phone. There was no phone booth near. He couldn't call for help. Ah, but it says he 'turned this way and that and saw that there was no one' (v. 12); so he must have been trying to sneak? But this idiom is used elsewhere, in Isaiah 59:16 (see also 63:5), where Yahweh 'sees there is no one,' meaning there was no one else around to help or intervene. So here, I take it, Moses turned this way and that to see if anyone *was* available to help and, seeing none, threw himself into the fray and liquidated the Egyptian. Did Moses act without a 'call' here? I don't know. Perhaps so. Certainly later, in chapters 3–4, when God clearly called him, Moses wanted no part of it; it was as if he had lost the vision for delivering Israel.[11] But as far as this isolated episode goes, I find it hard to fault Moses; it seems to me that if you find an Egyptian beating the tar out of an Israelite, it's a no-brainer.

But let's not get hung up on that dispute. Note what the text implies about Moses' motives: 'he went out to his brothers, and looked on their burdens, and he saw an Egyptian man beating a Hebrew man, one of his brothers' (v. 11). English translations tend to neuter the text – they get apoplexy it seems over masculine terms, so change the 'brother' to the generic 'people' or something similar. More on this in a moment. You remember the commentary of Hebrews 11:24-26? What weird values Moses has! Moses had every reason to look at things differently. He could have said he had his MA from Delta U. but that these Israelites were below sub-class; he had grown accustomed to a more refined culture and Israel lived such an outhouse style of life. But what matters to Moses? His 'brothers.' And there's a reason for my crotchety insistence on a literal translation. I'm not trying to be mystical, but doesn't seeing 'brothers' here in the Hebrew text conjure up in one's mind what Hebrews 2:11 and 17 say about Jesus? 'He is not ashamed to call them brothers.' 'He had to be made like his brothers in every respect.'[12]

We must also ask how we are to construe the incident with the two Hebrew men (vv. 13-14). The one in the wrong rejects Moses' 'justice' and intervention. Is the offender properly questioning Moses' authority? Note how Stephen interprets this incident in Acts 7:23-29 (+ 35), in which he sees an Israelite *pattern*, culminating in Israel's rejection of Jesus. One could say he draws a parallel between Moses' rejection here and Jesus' rejection by Israel in his own time. Stephen's interpretation of 2:13-14 would fit the pattern of Israel's rejecting or resisting Moses in Exodus (14:11-12; 16:2ff.; 17:1-7; 32:1-6). Whether we think Moses was operating without a divine call or not, this man, according to Stephen, was being the typical, vintage Israelite. He's of the seed of Abraham but wants no truck with a savior.

Moses' third attempt at bringing justice (vv. 15-21) seems to be completely successful and a little amusing. Reuel's daughters were probably used to getting harassed at the well (note his amazement, v. 18, over their being home at a decent time that particular day). What macho fellows these local shepherds were! They could drive away girls from watering their sheep – until they met a fellow who had the guts to take them on. It was as if a savior had been driven out of Egypt just for a bunch of helpless Midianite girls.[13]

Interim Comments on Exodus 2:11-22

We must move away now from the individual segments of this passage. In fact, you may find you don't agree with much I've said about them. No matter: We can still agree, I think, on the impact verses 11-22 are meant to make on us readers.

So we step back a bit from this passage and look at the whole landscape. Israel rots in Egypt, Moses is banished, and the only 'salvation' is for seven girls at a well in Midian. We are tempted to ask, 'Why this waste?' Verses 1-10 had gotten our hopes up, but verses 11-22 seem to negate the whole purpose of verses 1-10. As Ellison says:

> During the long years that followed it seemed as though all Moses' providential training had been for nothing. His first-class education was apparently being wasted as he devoted all his efforts to keeping a few sheep alive amid the sparse vegetation of a semi-desert land.[14]

Disappointment and futility seem to dog God's plans. Moses is marvelously spared, superbly educated – for finding pasture for sheep. God's foolishness rides again.

Observations on Exodus 2:23-25

I have an electric coffee-maker at home. It has a capacity to make 10-12 cups. It uses the 'drip' method. I fill a reservoir with water, the unit heats that water and spews it over a basket containing ground coffee, out of which the coffee then dribbles down into the carafe that sits on the hot plate below. Now my coffee-maker, plain as it is, nevertheless has a little shut-off mechanism. For example, if I am impatient and want to pour a cup of coffee before the whole amount has finished brewing, I simply pull the carafe out and the dripping from the brew basket stops; I fill my cup, return the carafe to its place, and the coffee, having been momentarily 'dammed up' in the brew basket, rushes with unaccustomed gusto into the carafe. Now that is my impression of Exodus 2:23-25. Throughout Exodus 1 and 2 it is as if almost any mention of God has been 'dammed up.' It seems like there is a conspiracy of silence about him. He is only mentioned three times in Exodus 1 toward the end of the chapter, and he never speaks. In all of 2:1-22 there is no reference to him at all. And then, as if pent up for all too long, in 2:23-25 references to God's activity come tumbling into the text: 'their cry for help... came up to God, and God heard...God remembered...God saw...and God knew.'[15]

Let us note one other item in this section. Verse 23 tells us that 'as those many days wore on, the king of Egypt died' and Israel still sighed and groaned under their slavery. In short, a change in political circumstances (death of a Pharaoh) made no difference in Israel's circumstances. Sometimes, it seems, it could. As Sarna explains:

> It was established practice in Egypt for a new king to celebrate his accession to the throne by granting amnesty to

those guilty of crimes, by releasing prisoners, and by freeing slaves. An extant hymn composed in honor of the accession of Ramses IV illustrates the custom. It records 'a happy day' for Egypt when 'fugitives returned to their towns' and when 'those in hiding emerged' and 'those in prison were freed.' This being so, the Israelites had good reason to expect that the change in regime would bring with it some amelioration of their condition. But this was not to be. Hence the stress on the intensified misery of the enslaved Israelites.[16]

In this way the text preaches where genuine hope can be found: not in political change but in divine faithfulness.

Exposition of Exodus 2

A leader of a mob of Hindu extremists, at the invitation of the police, addresses two Christians who were visiting a home worship service in central India. He tells them that if they come again their bones will be broken and they will be burned alive. Christian girls and young women in Pakistan are kidnapped, raped, pressured to convert to Islam; churches and Christian homes in Alexandria, Egypt, are attacked by angry Muslim mobs; three Christian school girls are beheaded by machete-wielding thugs in Indonesia; converts to Christ in Uzbekistan are publicly humiliated and even denied access to drinking water. On and on goes the litany of the suffering people of God in our own day. Christ's people are so often a suffering people. Pharaoh is legion and apparently alive and well.

Some of us may not currently be in the grip of unjust oppression. But Jesus has told us what the 'norm' is (Mark 13:13). And Exodus 2 certainly provides us with a clear sample. Here are the people God will take to be his very own people and yet they are trampled and beaten down. How can such people have hope? Why can such people have hope?

It seems to me that Exodus 2 answers that question. Obviously, the chapter can be preached in its individual segments, but taking the chapter as a whole provides us with the reasons for finding in God 'our hope for years to come.'

The text teaches that God's people have hope *because God preserves his people by his delightful providence* (vv. 1-10). By 'providence' here I simply mean that always interesting way God rules and twists circumstances to his people's welfare. I shan't go over again all the ground we've already covered on 2:1-10. But here is a mother who does all she can humanly do (vv. 3-4). She may have watched the movements of Pharaoh's daughter for some time. It was a desperate scheme and yet she hadn't many options. Perhaps (as noted in chapter 2) she was hoping Pharaoh's daughter's paganism would even assist: if she found a Hebrew lad safely nestled in the Nile, would she 'divine' that the Nile god must be protecting him? Who knows? But here in this section is all the calculation and desperation of a mother, all the tension of a sister's watching (v. 4) and a princess's discovery (vv. 5-6), the humor as a monarch's decree is frustrated (vv. 7-10; see previous discussion), and the fascination of a God who is never mentioned yet seems so incontrovertibly there. God reveals himself as interesting and hilarious and unobtrusive all in one episode.

Still we do well to acknowledge the mystery. Some will surely think of the difficulty. Baby Moses is spared but doubtless there were any number of other Hebrew baby boys that Egyptians chucked to Davy Jones' locker in the bottom of the Nile. A 'Moses experience' was likely the rare exception. God did not specially save all Hebrew boys but saved the one who would be savior of his people (just as in Matthew 2:13-23 not every Bethlehem toddler was saved, but the Savior was saved). Maybe all this helps us to see what God's promise to us really is: he does not promise that his people will never suffer but that no suffering will ever eradicate his people; he does not promise that we will never die for the kingdom of God but that the kingdom of God will never die. Here God preserves one baby boy who in turn will be the deliverer for God's whole people. The promise of the text is that God *will* always have a people to serve him on this earth – and there's no earthly tyrant who can stop him. God has his ways – amusing, quiet ways – of making sure of that.

Secondly, I would take up verses 11-22 as a whole and emphasize that God's people have hope *because God overrules his servants' disappointments for their good*. The action in this section moves from sympathy (v. 11a) to action (vv. 11b-12) to rejection (vv. 13-14) to exile (vv. 15ff.). Even in Midian, however, Moses is a deliverer, seeking to bring justice even if only for a bunch of intimidated girls. However, precisely at this point it looks like all that marvelous providence in verses 1-10 has gone for nothing. All Moses' efforts have ended in yuck; one mess after another; a series of disappointments. He has his MA in Government Administration and ends up doing blue collar work in the bleak stretches of the Sinai peninsula. Does that make sense? Is this the foolishness of God?

Hardly. Consider some matters (even if they are, in part, over, under, and around the text): (1) Years later Moses would have to lead Israel through the area of Sinai; would not his thorough knowledge of it (cf. 3:1) prove a huge advantage? (2) The 'Midian connection' will lead to the eventual conversion of Moses' father-in-law (Reuel/Jethro) to Yahweh (Exod. 18; see our discussion back in chapter 6); is that not worth some trouble? (3) His disappointment and exile will develop an empathy for his people's misery and condition. On this last matter, Moshe Greenberg states: 'Without the long exile in Midian he would not have experienced even a semblance of the alienness that was his people's lot in Egypt.'[17] It was commendable for Moses to walk out of posh government service to seek to deliver his people. But what experience had he had of their hardships? What did he know of being looked on as an alien? Perhaps Moses' suffering was necessary preparation for helping a suffering people (cf. 2 Cor. 1:3-4). Maybe Midian wasn't madness after all. Maybe God's invisible wisdom was mixed with his apparent foolishness.

J. B. and Vera Phillips were living and ministering in south-east London and trying to live through the German bombings in those earlier World War II years. During the time of the night bombings they usually walked through two back gardens to join an elderly couple whose kitchen table served as their joint nightly refuge. One evening they were on their way to this couple's place but decided to go the front way, by the pavement, in order to mail a letter at the corner post box. They knew the latest mail collection had already been made but both agreed they would post the letter that night anyway. No sooner had they done so than they heard the whistling whine of a stick of bombs. They flung themselves to the pavement, which shuddered, practically coming up to thump them on their chins. There was a deafening roar of an exploding bomb near-by. After staying prone until the attack seemed over, they got up and went to join their friends. It was then they were informed that there was now a crater some twenty feet across and seven deep in the back garden along the path they would normally have taken.[18] Why a seemingly trivial and unnecessary decision to go the front way and post a letter? Makes little sense, until one figures it out after the dust settles.

Isn't this really the same point Romans 8:28-29 presses upon us? Remember the 'good' in verse 28 is defined as being likeness to Christ in verse 29. Is this not how we are to look at all our shattered dreams, apparent failures, and heart-wrenching disappointments? When the wash is all in and the dust settles, there will not be anything that God has not used to shape us to the likeness of his Son.

Verses 23-25 give God's beaten people a third reason for hope – *because God never abandons his covenant promises.* Here I would want to show how different this concluding section is from all of Exodus 1–2 to this point – the reticence in even referring to God versus the rapid-fire, 'God + verb' clauses in verses 24-25 (God heard, God remembered, God saw, God knew). I would want to point out the contrast between an empty hope (political change, Pharaoh's death) and a true one (God's activity). All of the God-plus-verb clauses are rich; I might focus on 'And God remembered his covenant...' in 24b. What does it mean to 'remember' a covenant? Well, to remember promises made in such a covenant. What promises? Why, to give the land to Abraham's seed (Gen. 12), to bring them out of bondage in order to enjoy that land (Gen. 15), and to be God to Abraham's seed (Gen. 17), among others. But God's promises here are hundreds of years old! That's something the Christian knows about. But the text is saying to Israel and to us, 'Your hope is not in the death of a Pharaoh but in the covenant of God, not in some fortunate change in your condition but in the God who hears and remembers and sees and knows.' Sometimes it's only when our false hopes fail that we cast ourselves on our only hope. As a Christian, that is my position. When everything is whittled down to the stump, all I have are the old promises of my Savior (e.g., John 6:37, 40; 10:27-28; 14:3).

I can't help being partial to the story about John Brown of Haddington visiting one of his parishioners. She was on her death-bed and Brown was probing for her assurance. 'Janet,' he asked, 'what would you say if, after all He has done for you, God should let you drop into hell?' 'E'ens He likes,' came the answer, 'if He does, He'll lose mair than I'll do.'[19] 'Even as He likes; if He does, He'll lose more than I will.' (I would lose my soul; he would lose his reputation). That's called bedrock. Why don't we let Janet have the last word? That's a splendid note on which to end a book!

Endnotes

1. Many assume that the midwives 'storied' to Pharaoh, at least to some degree. Actually, we can't know that – we have to read that into their words. (Maybe it's a correct 'read-in' but we simply don't know). Why make a problem if we don't need to do so? When the midwives call the Hebrew women 'lively' or 'vigorous,' they use a term related to that for animals or wild beasts. It may be they are saying the Hebrew women are 'beasts' (cf. W. H. Gispen, *Exodus*, Bible Student's Commentary [Grand Rapids: Zondervan, 1982], 37). 'Look, Pharaoh, those women are like animals; they're not soft pansies like Egyptian women; they don't really need midwives.'

2. The writer shows how very bleak the situation is in verses 13-14 by ringing the changes on the 'slave' word (root = *'abad*) – five times in the Hebrew text.

3. J. A. Motyer, *The Message of Exodus*, The Bible Speaks Today (Downers Grove: InterVarsity, 2005), 32.

4. Gispen, *Exodus*, 31.

5. Nahum M. Sarna, *Exodus*, The JPS Torah Commentary (Philadelphia: Jewish Publication Society, 1991), 7.

6. The thrust of those promises (Gen. 12:2, 15:5, 17:6, etc.) is that there will be a covenant people in this world. Is not Jesus' 'I will build my church' (Matt. 16:18) a re-assertion of the same promise?

7. Sarna, *Exploring Exodus* (New York: Schocken, 1986), 25.

8. The midwives also instruct us on the secret of freedom (v. 17a): fear of God banishes all other fear.

9. The point still holds even if she was the adolescent offspring of some haremed wife some ways down on the royal preference totem-pole; cf. Sarna, *Exploring Exodus*, 31, and John D. Currid, *A Study Commentary on Exodus*, 2 vols. (Darlington: Evangelical Press, 2000), 1:61.

10. My friend and former colleague, John Currid, is likely still appalled that I should think so; see his *Study Commentary on Exodus*, 1:67; I am following some of Moshe Greenberg's discussion (*Understanding Exodus* [New York: Behrman House, 1969], 44-45).

11. See especially, Motyer, *The Message of Exodus*, 59-62.

12. How different from the typical great ones of the world. For example, Paul Johnson points out how Lenin 'never visited a factory or set foot on a farm' and was never seen in the working-class quarters of any town where he resided. 'His entire life was spent among the members of his own sub-class, the bourgeois intelligentsia' (*Modern Times*, rev. ed. [New York: Harper Perennial, 1992], 52). So much for a champion of the workers.

13. I will not discuss the admittedly significant naming of Gershom in verse 22 – because I'm not sure what it means. The cognate verb root (*grs*) is used in verse 17 when the shepherds drive away Reuel's daughters. Perhaps the text suggests that Moses is one who has been 'driven away' from Egypt to Midian. In any case, the word-play explanation Moses gives is that he has been a 'sojourner' (*gēr*) in a foreign land, the name standing for 'a sojourner there.' The tricky part is to know where 'there' is. Is he referring to Midian where he now is? Is he referring to Egypt where he had been? Is he saying he doesn't belong in Midian or that he never belonged in Egypt? Cf. John L. Mackay, *Exodus* (Ross-shire: Christian Focus, 2001), 60-61; and Sarna, *Exodus*, JPS Torah Commentary, 12-13.

14. H. L. Ellison, *Exodus*, Daily Study Bible (Philadelphia: Westminster, 1982), 12-13.

15. See Motyer, *The Message of Exodus*, 41, for the difference one meets at 2:23ff. (his section is 'False starts and true beginnings').

16. *Exodus*, JPS Commentary, 13.

17. *Understanding Exodus*, 49.

18. J. B. Phillips, *The Price of Success* (Wheaton: Harold Shaw, 1984), 96-97.

19. Robert Mackenzie, *John Brown of Haddington* (London: Hodder and Stoughton, 1918), 101-102.